Soviet Images of America

Stephen P. Gibert

CONTRIBUTING AUTHORS

Arthur A. Zuehlke, Jr.

Richard Soll

Michael J. Deane

Crane, Russak & Company, Inc.

NEW YORK

Contents

Commentary

Soviet-American relations can be described as a competition between systems encompassing a wide range of political, military, economic, social, ideological, and scientific-technological interactions. The psychological dimension of this relationship, although not readily apparent in the rhetoric and actions of the superpowers, is nevertheless fundamental and determining. The policies and behavior of the United States and the Soviet Union proceed according to the images their national decisionmakers hold of themselves, their adversaries, and the global environment in which they coexist. These images are formed through experience and possess significant inertia: that is to say, the basic images of an adversary change only very gradually, if at all. Since such images function, if you will, as a prism through which a decisionmaker views events and determines a course of action, understanding their content is of vital importance to efforts at forecasting a nation-state's behavior. These propositions apply especially to Soviet leaders, whose images of the West and the United States in particular are nurtured by Marxism-Leninism and tempered by the Soviet Union's sixty years of experience in an international arena perceived to be hostile to Russian interests.

In my judgment, recent foreign policy behavior of the USSR is quite consistent with the Soviet images of the United States revealed in this study. These views show great vitality and continuity with past expressions. The leaders of the CPSU have over recent decades clearly stated their intentions toward the West, outlined the guiding

i

principles of their foreign policy, and engaged in comprehensive assessments of the trends of world politics. More often than not, Western analysts have seen fit to dismiss such articulations as propaganda and bombast or mere "lip-service" to an ideology devoid of foreign policy relevance. Dean Acheson bemoaned this fact in his work *Power and Diplomacy* nearly twenty years ago:

> No matter how plainly the Russians talk and act, we simply refuse to believe what they say and to understand the meaning of what they do. President Eisenhower and Secretary Dulles keep insisting that the test must be deeds not words. Floods of deeds follow, amply explained by torrents of words. Yet our leaders and, indeed, our people cannot believe what they see and hear.

The issue of détente between the United States and the USSR has illustrated most vividly the difficulty Americans appear to have in understanding the Soviet Union. The concept of détente represented quite different notions to Washington than it did to the Kremlin. Détente or peaceful coexistence was candidly explained in the Soviet press as an offensive policy, a strategem for dealing with the West, the chief value of which stemmed from the fact that it helped reduce the likelihood of a mutually destructive nuclear war. On this basis there was little misunderstanding between East and West. Yet détente meant a good deal more to the Soviets. The struggle against capitalism on all fronts was to continue unabated. In fact, under conditions of détente, Soviet leaders called for heightening the ideological struggle and pledged anew their support for national liberation movements. As the events of the Vietnam War, the Middle East War of October 1973, and, most recently, the victory of the MPLA in Angola, indicate, détente has in no way altered the Soviet commitment to victory in the struggle with the West, and restrained neither their words nor their deeds. This aggressive Soviet behavior pursued under "détente," or the "relaxation of tensions" becomes understandable in light of the perception of the Kremlin that détente is based on a necessary Western accommodation to growing Soviet power and the gains of world socialism. Soviet spokesmen assert that Washington's willingness to enter into détente is a manifestation of weakness. The alleged victories in the world-wide "national liberation struggle," the American failure in

Vietnam, the approaching "crisis" in Western economic systems, the internal "contradictions" of "bourgeois society," the achievement of strategic military parity by the USSR—these and other phenomena (both fanciful and real) are viewed as important components contributing to a "shift in the world correlation of forces" in the favor of the USSR, providing evidence for the inevitable future worldwide victory of socialism. Thus détente is intended to prevent nuclear war between the two superpowers while the correlation of forces—defined in the international arena as the total of ideological, economic, political and military factors which constitute the fund of power of opposing groups of nations—continues to enhance the position of the Soviet Union vis-à-vis the United States. Détente, accordingly, is "reversible" while the correlation of forces is not.

Given Moscow's image of a weakening United States and capitalist West increasingly unable to meet the Soviet challenge in the intersystemic contest of wills, it is small wonder that, as Soviet capabilities grow vis-à-vis the West, the Kremlin now seeks to operationalize policies that in the past appeared to Americans as mere rhetoric. It is now of vital importance for the national security of the United States that the USSR not only perceive America's capability to defend its interests throughout the world but also recognize America's willingness to confront whatever risks may be involved in doing so.

This study, through its careful documentation from open Russian sources, maps both the contours and specific features of Soviet images of America and its role in world affairs. It provides an important vantage point to those engaged in the task of analyzing Soviet foreign policy, illuminating Soviet perspectives of the West. It thus serves as a check against that persistent problem hindering Western analyses—the tendency to "mirror image" the Russians, or unconsciously ascribe Western values and concepts to the decision-makers of the USSR.

The research for this book was undertaken at the Stanford Research Institute's Strategic Studies Center in Rosslyn, Virginia. The Center is especially well-equipped for analyses of Soviet foreign policy, Soviet military strategy and doctrine, and the Soviet economy. The Center's Russian-language library holds more than six thousand volumes, subscribes to approximately fifty Soviet periodicals in political, military, and economic subject areas, and maintains major Soviet reference series. To these resources are added an experienced staff and the Center's valuable work spanning two decades which includes a wide spectrum of Russian area research. Among the recent studies conducted by the Center are studies of Soviet-American competition in the Middle East, détente, Soviet strategy in Europe, Soviet policy toward the Third World, and the role of social science research institutes in the formulation and execution of Soviet foreign policy. Particularly useful in enhancing the Strategic Studies Center's comprehension of the substance and process of Soviet foreign policy and strategy toward the West has been the dialogue maintained through a series of symposia between the Center and two Soviet research institutions, the Institute of World Economy and International Relations (IMEMO) and the Institute for the Study of the United States and Canada (IUSAC).

This book grew out of a research project intended to further the understanding of present Soviet-American relations. Stephen P. Gibert, a Professor of Government at Georgetown University, who has contributed frequently to SRI studies on superpower interrelationships and United States and Soviet foreign policy, was asked to lead the project. Dr. Gibert was particularly suitable since his principal academic interest is Soviet-American relations. Subsequently, Professor Gibert and several of the original study group decided to further explore the subject. This book is the product of their additional effort.

Dr. Gibert's principal collaborator in this book was Arthur A. Zuehlke, Jr., a Fellow in the Department of Government at Georgetown University and Research Analyst at SRI's Strategic Studies Center. Mr. Zuehlke is a specialist in Soviet studies and international politics.

Particular mention should be made of Richard Soll, formerly of SRI and now a defense analyst specializing in Soviet studies at the Systems Planning Corporation. While Mr. Soll did not participate in the expanded effort which resulted in this book, many of his contributions to the original study have been preserved in the finished work.

Dr. Michael J. Deane, a young scholar who formerly was a Soviet specialist on the SRI staff, although not a member of the original study team, joined Dr. Gibert and Mr. Zuehlke in the additional research and analysis required which culminated in this work.

While this book was produced with the support of SRI, the arguments and views presented are those of the authors alone and do not necessarily reflect those of the Strategic Studies Center or myself, although we find substantial areas of agreement. Its unifying theme concerns détente: What do Soviet views of the United States tell us about détente and the future of Soviet-American relations? This is the single most important question in international politics today.

In this era, when an even greater number of Americans are undertaking a serious reassessment of U.S. foreign policy, it is hoped this book will make a valuable and informative contribution to that process. The analysis of Soviet images of the United States presented in this book perhaps will offer us that insight so nicely summarized by Robert Burns:

> Oh wad some power the giftie gie us
> To see oursels as others see us
> It wad frae monie a blunder free us
>   An' foolish notion

Richard B. Foster
Director, Strategic Studies
Center
Stanford Research Institute

Acknowledgments

Among American observers of the Soviet Union there is a growing consensus that Soviet military capabilities are enormous and well beyond those required for purely defensive purposes. Further, it appears that Soviet leaders have rejected the concept of superpower parity in favor of attempting to acquire a politically useful margin of military superiority over the United States. More ambiguous, however, are Moscow's intentions: Just what do Soviet leaders intend to do in world politics? How do they—in the present era of nuclear parity—see the future of Soviet-American relations? How, in fact, do they view America generally? Does peaceful coexistence mean that it may be anticipated that competition between the United States and the Soviet Union will be gradually replaced with a more mutually beneficial relationship? Or does the Soviet government intend to use peaceful coexistence to lessen the risks of nuclear conflict while aggressively pursuing competition in all other aspects of superpower interactions?

These and other questions obviously cannot be answered definitively in this book. It is hoped, however, that the detailed analysis of Soviet statements about the United States and its role in international affairs presented here will contribute partial answers to these questions. For, although it has become fashionable to elevate American relations with the Third World to the center of foreign policy attention, the awesome power commanded by both the Soviet Union and the United States ensures that Soviet-American relations will remain the dominant international political problem for the remainder of this century. It is this conviction that led to the writing of this book.

Any author who writes on foreign policy and national security affairs owes an intellectual debt to many people. This is especially true in the case of this book since it would have been next to impossible for one person to assemble and analyze the vast amounts of data required. Also, of course, since this study deals with the perspectives of Soviet decision-makers (and not merely overt policy actions), it was extremely useful to get a variety of opinions on the subjects concerned. My first debt is to two of the three contributing authors, Arthur A. Zuehlke and Richard Soll. Zuehlke and Soll translated hundreds of Soviet statements, speeches, and articles. In some cases these were already available in translation and our translations were compared with those to ensure that subtle nuances had not been missed. In other cases, material utilized here was available only in the Russian.

Subsequently, Zuehlke, Soll, and I spent many hours sifting through this material to try to make certain that views selected for inclusion indeed represented authoritative Soviet opinion. Finally, we subjected the remaining data to a systematic content analysis to derive appropriate interpretations.

When the time came to analyze the Twenty-fifth Congress of the CPSU, Soll's place was taken by Michael Deane, the third contributing author. I am grateful for his efforts.

Several other persons assisted me in various ways. Paul Holman contributed ideas and commentary for the third chapter. William Carpenter and Harold Silverstein read the entire manuscript and made many editorial suggestions. Leon Goure and Walter Laqueur were also kind enough to critique the manuscript and it doubtless was improved because of their efforts. I am grateful also to Richard Foster, the Director of the Strategic Studies Center of Stanford Research Institute and to Ben Russak of Crane, Russak and Co., Inc., who encouraged this publication.

Finally, Georgetown University granted me a sabbatical leave in the spring of 1976 which permitted me the necessary time to complete this book.

Stephen P. Gibert

Image and Reality in Superpower Policy

FAULTY perceptions of the policies of other nations or of the motives, beliefs and actions of their leaders and people can and do lead to disastrous mistakes. A few examples will suffice:

- In the fall of 1941, because the United States had broken the Japanese diplomatic code, American leaders knew that the Japanese government was acquiring detailed information about Pearl Harbor, including the berthing of American warships. But these U.S. officials were so convinced Japan would not attack Pearl Harbor that this indication that the Japanese might be preparing a military attack was perceived as merely "Japanese diligence."

- Secretary of State Dulles perceived America's enemy to be international communism, not the Soviet Union. This perception led to the massive retaliation theory which had as a central idea the concept of monolithic communism; the United States was thus blinded to growing evidence of disarray and eventually conflict in the Sino-Soviet bloc.

- In 1961 the Cuban people were seen as extremely displeased with the Castro regime. This perception played an important role in the Bay of Pigs disaster. Related to this was Premier Khrushchev's perception of President Kennedy as inexperienced, weak and indecisive, which was to lead ultimately to the Cuban missile crisis.

- The Israelis were convinced in the summer of 1973 that the Egyptians could not mount a successful attack across the Suez Canal; this perception played an important role in the intelligence failure at the beginning of the Yom Kippur War.

Examples abound of perceptual errors leading to incorrect foreign policy choices. But it is not only distorted views of reality that make the subject of Soviet perceptions important. On the contrary, it may be even more useful to know the correct perceptions which Soviet leaders hold of the United States.

- The Soviet government correctly perceived that the United States and its NATO allies, both in 1956 and in 1968, were not willing to run whatever risks would have been entailed in supporting emerging anti-Warsaw Treaty Organization regimes in Eastern Europe. Hence the Soviet leadership utilized military force to suppress those regimes and installed governments more subject to their control in Budapest and Prague.

- Despite the Soviet introduction of offensive missiles into Cuba in 1962, the USSR was well aware that at both the strategic and tactical level the United States possessed military superiority. Rather than challenge the United States under such conditions, the USSR withdrew its missiles in the face of a U.S. ultimatum and accepted a substantial political defeat.

- Moscow also correctly perceived that the U.S. government, for a variety of reasons, would not take action to prevent or counterbalance a massive resupply of the North Vietnamese-Viet Cong forces after the "truce" of 1973. Hence modern weapons of the most sophisticated sort were sent to the Communist armies in South Vietnam, contributing substantially to their final victory in 1975.

Thus, whether or not Soviet perceptions represent a correct view of the United States, a full comprehension of such perceptions by American national security decisionmakers will make more explicable the foreign policies pursued by the Soviet Union.

The Perceptual Process

The perceptual process involves acquiring, classifying, evaluating and integrating or rejecting information. Of course, the decision-maker is not a "blank slate"; he already has a number of assumptions and beliefs about the world which he has acquired over the years.

Although images, both of one's own nation and of the external world, are oversimplified ard tend to be stereotyped, they do perform the valuable task of "making sense" out of a plethora of seemingly unrelated or only partially related events. Naturally, the belief system is not neutral; it finds it easier to accept political communications which confirm existing notions of reality and is less inclined to accept information which contradicts or requires the modification of existing images of the world. It is this psychological predisposition which makes it very difficult to change perceptions. With regard to Russian perceptions, however, it may be possible to affect those views which do not lie at the core of their national self-image and are not fundamental to the Marxist-Leninist belief system. And, of course, just as some people are more receptive to religious teachings than others, so also can it be assumed that convictions about communism and its apocalyptic view of the future vary among Soviet leaders. Thus, while an overly optimistic view of modifying Soviet perceptions about the United States and its role in world affairs should be rejected, some success with at least some Soviet leaders should be anticipated. For this reason, an understanding of Soviet perceptions not only will lead to a better comprehension of the foreign policy of the USSR, but also will make it possible for national security decisionmakers to improve the position of the United States in the ongoing competitive struggle with the USSR. Appropriate policies to affect Soviet perceptions, however, must rest on at least a rudimentary knowledge of the theory of international perceptions. Social scientists have constructed such a theory by taking concepts from social and behavioral psychology and applying them to political situations in order to attempt to understand the foreign policies of nation-states.[1]

The first component in the perceptual process is referred to as the cognitive, or the discerning of factual reality. Factual reality is that part of understanding on the part of the decisionmaker which stems from experience and common sense; certain things are obviously true and others false. However, this is not a sufficient guide to action, for at any moment the decisionmaker may be confronted with

---

[1] An excellent reader concerned with perceptions analysis, attitude formation and the interrelationship of political "images" and foreign policy behavior is Herbert C. Kelman, ed., *International Behavior: A Social-Psychological Analysis* (New York: Holt, Rinehart and Winston, 1965).

hundreds of facts from which he must make a selection on which to act. A few facts become crucial, others are discarded, some are not recognized in the first place. Reality, in short, consists of an enormous amount of information, of which only a very small fraction can enter into the calculations of the decisionmaker. He must scan the universe, select the most salient facts and array them logically in his mind in such a way that they give him a sufficient grasp of reality to make logical choices.

Earlier theorists of international relations assumed that decisional choices were both logical and optimal; what has been referred to as the "rational actor model" of foreign policy behavior was accepted.[2] In contrast, perceptions theory rejects the notion of a totally "rational" foreign policy. In place of *Homo politicus* they substitute a more complex theory of how decisionmakers view the world and how, accordingly, nations behave. Thus it is not sufficient to describe the cognitive or factual reality component of perceptions; it is also necessary to take into account the process by which certain facts are selected and others not, as well as the psychological orientation of the decisionmaker toward factual reality. Two elements in addition to cognitions in the perceptual process have been identified. These are referred to as values and beliefs.

Values refer to preferences on the part of the decisionmaker. He may prefer Israelis to Arabs, Greeks to Turks, India to Pakistan. These values (or, to use a pejorative term, prejudices) may have been acquired over a lifetime. On the other hand, a particular preference may reflect institutional affiliation or may be related to personal career advancement. Thus the decisionmaker is not neutral when he selects information upon which to construct his "factual reality." Rather, he selects "facts" which tend to reinforce or at least not disturb his own set of preferences. Contrary information is likely not to be noticed or may be discarded as false or irrelevant.

Beliefs are convictions that a particular description of reality is true, proved and (usually) obvious. Thus democratic governments are seen as less inclined to war than dictatorships; peace, not war, is "normal"; conflicts between nations result from lack of understand-

---

2 For a discussion of the "rational actor model" and two other "conceptual models" used in an attempt to explain American policy during the 1962 Cuban missile crisis, see Graham T. Allison, *Essence of Decision* (Boston: Little, Brown and Company, 1971).

ing among peoples; and so on. Again, if a belief conflicts with contrary data, this information is likely to be ignored or its validity denied.

To sum up the three aspects of perception: a cognition is data or information received from the environment, a value specifies not what is true but a preference for what ought to be true (sometimes referred to as affective orientation) and a belief is a conviction that a particular description of reality is indeed correct. Taken together, the three elements, along with past and current behavior, form the attitudinal basis for political action and constitute the process by which decisionmakers form images of their own country, the international environment and other nation-states.

The Soviet World View

Russian perceptions of the United States are conditioned by the Soviet leaders' images of their own country, the United States and the world in general. While it is not possible to investigate the belief systems of individual members of the Soviet ruling hierarchy, it is feasible to describe the general world view to which all Soviet leaders are exposed and which constitutes an important element in their political socialization as they climb to positions of power in the USSR.[3]

The fundamental tenet of the Soviet belief system is the view that social development is a natural evolutionary process whereby mankind moves through historical stages until it reaches the final stage of communism. Thus the Soviet view of society is a dynamic one, which holds that all social systems are constantly changing. While the force propelling society toward its predetermined destiny is that of the class struggle, it is the duty of the Soviet elite to guide and

---

[3] It is not intended here to describe in detail the basic tenets, now familiar to most Western observers of the USSR, of Marxism-Leninism. Rather, it is the objective of this section to focus briefly on the teleological or goal-oriented features of Soviet doctrine, with special emphasis upon those aspects considered fundamental to understanding Soviet perceptions of the United States and its role in world affairs. For readers interested in pursuing the subject of Marxism-Leninism, convenient anthologies have been published in English. See *Karl Marx and Frederick Engels: Selected Works,* 3 vols. (Moscow: Progress Publishers, 1969-70); *The Fundamentals of Marxist-Leninist Philosophy* (Moscow: Progress Publishers, 1974); and *Lenin: Selected Works,* 3 vols. (Moscow: Progress Publishers, 1970-71).

manage social change, thus hastening the evolutionary process and safeguarding the socialist homeland until capitalist imperialism finally disappears.

This view of the world profoundly affects Soviet perceptions:

- Soviet leaders see themselves as "men of the future"; leaders of the West are "men of the past."

- Russia's elites are confident that communism will ultimately prevail. There is no need, accordingly, to take unnecessary risks.

- Soviet decisionmakers "naturally" accord high priority to long-range planning, to the study of the future. In contrast, their world view leads them to expect U.S. leaders to be more concerned with improvisation, the "quick-fix," and the present and immediate as distinct from the more distant future.

- Nuclear war is to be avoided, but Soviet leaders are confident that should it occur the USSR will survive and capitalism will be destroyed. Thus the Soviet government prepares constantly for the possibility of a war in which all weapons of mass destruction are to be utilized without restraint.

A second important component of the Soviet world image is the organic view of society; society is a "living organism" in its functioning and in its development. This element also affects Soviet perceptions in several particulars:

- Social development follows objective laws. Integrative principles have an objective character independent of human consciousness or will.

- It is possible to develop a complete understanding of reality by means of a systemic approach; everything has its own inner logic, best comprehended through dialectical methods of reasoning.

- Management of global change can be accomplished by the Soviet leaders since they understand the origins, development and direction of social forces. Such an understanding reveals that trends in the United States are leading to its eventual dissolution and demise.

A third fundamental element of the Soviet world view is derived from Lenin: imperialism is the highest stage of capitalism and capitalism is at its most dangerous in this phase. This concept affects Soviet perceptions in very significant ways:

- The United States, although progressively growing weaker, is still quite dangerous and to be treated cautiously. Détente can lessen the danger of war during this period of the waning of capitalism.

- Basically, as men of the past, American leaders are not altogether rational and predictable. A partial explanation for this unpredictability is that the ruling classes have lost confidence in their ability to govern.

- The United States can have no altruistic policies in the Third World; all are intended, in one way or another, to restore the Third World as an area for capitalist exploitation.

- Rivalry between the United States and other capitalist nations is bound to exist, as each attempts to carve out areas in the Third World for exploitation. Thus it should be possible to weaken America's alliances with Western Europe and Japan.

A fourth fundamental aspect of the Soviet world view is the theory of revolution. Revolution is said to occur in the wake of wars or severe depressions or other great crises. The Communist vanguard, recognizing that "objective factors" are favorable, successfully exploit the situation. This concept also affects Soviet perceptions in various ways:

- Soviet spokesmen are especially receptive to events that could be called a crisis; they constantly "look for" such objective situations and, accordingly, tend to overemphasize the seriousness of many of the problems they perceive.

- Soviet leaders also look for (and therefore tend to discover) potential revolutionary elements, including specific persons, in non-Communist societies who might put themselves at the service of Soviet purposes.

- Revolutionary "adventurism" is discouraged. This means that the Soviets may tend to perceive a genuine revolution as occurring "too early"; if the objective conditions are not ripe, attempts to move too fast may backfire and result in a fascist or right-wing regime rather than a Communist one. This belief tends to contribute to Soviet caution, both in terms of perceptions and in terms of exploiting new situations.

- While an adventurist policy is not favored, at the same time Soviet leaders may misinterpret the "objective factors" in specific situations and believe that they can move with impunity against the capitalist world. In such cases, Soviet policy assumes a bolder and more aggressive character and confrontation may result.

These Marxist-Leninist beliefs constitute the most coherent and organized components of the Soviet world view. Undoubtedly, however, there are other aspects of the Soviet world view which affect Soviet perceptions but about which it is difficult to speculate. These include elements derived from the Russian heritage, such as geopolitical determinism, Pan-Slavism and empire-building propensities.

It is likely also that psychological characteristics of Soviet leaders affect their world view. Some of those characteristics may be peculiar to the personality of a given leader. Other psychological aspects, however, may be derived from the cultural heritage. This latter phenomenon, generally referred to as "national character," also undoubtedly influences the ways in which Soviet leaders view the world. However, being more inchoate, not institutionalized and lacking official sanction, these components of the world view may not have an impact upon Soviet perceptions to the same degree or constitute an established element of the political culture as does the Marxist-Leninist framework. By comparison, Marxism-Leninism provides Soviet leaders with intellectual guidelines, furnishes methods for analyzing problems, justifies strategies and tactics and establishes a set of long-range foreign policy goals. Finally—and most importantly—Marxism-Leninism also helps define and give content to that nebulous concept known as "national interest."

Analyzing Soviet Perceptions: Some Methodological Problems

A fundamental controversy has existed for many years among American specialists on the Soviet Union as to the credence one can place on Soviet statements and published views. Certainly, to the extent that it is possible, Soviet views must be weighed carefully against policy and other kinds of evidence to try to determine which pronouncements in fact represent those true perceptions which condition Soviet strategy and foreign policy. Accordingly, an attempt has been made to differentiate between those Soviet authoritative statements which probably do not represent genuine Soviet beliefs and those that do.

This is not to suggest that the study of stated views, even if not "believed" by the spokesmen themselves, is not important. On the contrary, Soviet pronouncements about the United States serve a variety of useful purposes. A Soviet statement, for example, may be a "signal" to elicit a desired response from the United States. Soviet insistence that the U.S. forward-based systems (FBS) be included in SALT I, presumably because these systems posed a strategic-military threat to the USSR, apparently constituted a device for Soviet bargaining leverage as well as a stratagem to exacerbate difficulties in the NATO alliance. The subsequent dropping of their insistence on including FBS in the overall totals agreed to at Vladivostok seems to indicate that such assertions on FBS did not reflect Soviet perceptions of a significant threat from these systems.

It must also be borne in mind that Soviet views about the United States, especially those broadcast or published in open sources, reach many different audiences. These include groups within the Soviet Union, the COMECON nations, the People's Republic of China, Japan, Western Europe, the Third World and the United States. A statement, in the case of the Soviet audience, may serve the process of political socialization or a legitimizing function for the Soviet elite. Also, Soviet articulations are components of the network of communications by which the Soviet ruling elite informs the state and party apparatus and provides guidance and coherence to its vast and complex political and economic structure. Publicly expressed views about such issues as the presence of American troops in Western Europe may be intended to exacerbate differences in the United States between the Congress and the Administration on this point or to lend encouragement to groups in Europe who oppose the stationing of American soldiers in their countries. It must be remembered, in short, that words can be used to accomplish political goals.[4]

Illustrative examples of articulations apparently intended to serve propagandistic or other purposes and which appear not to represent true perceptions are noted below:

---

[4] This point is convincingly argued in Thomas M. Franck and Edward Weisband, *Word Politics: Verbal Strategy among the Superpowers* (New York: Oxford University Press, 1972).

- The United States accepted a relationship with the USSR based upon principles of peaceful coexistence because it was "forced" into this position by recognition of Soviet strength.

- U.S.-Soviet trade is of greater benefit to the United States than to the Soviet Union.

- U.S. acceptance of the principles of peaceful coexistence, as defined by the Soviets, will help to ameliorate U.S. relations with Western and Third World countries.

- The People's Republic of China has consistently since 1963, attempted to undermine East-West peaceful coexistence and obstruct the world Communist and national liberation movements.

Some Soviet utterances clearly are intended to serve the immediate needs of the moment and probably do not represent true Soviet beliefs. Other statements are inconsistent with the general thrust of Soviet foreign policy. Accordingly, in this study, authoritative Soviet pronouncements concerning the United States and its role in world affairs were placed in the total context in which they occurred. Judgments then were made as to which views represented articulations and which were perceptions.

Several observations need to be made concerning this approach.[5] First, when the occasional statement or the one which does not "fit the pattern" is screened out, Soviet views tend to be presented here as more homogeneous than is warranted. While it is the case that on all important issues Soviet public utterances do follow strict guidelines, there is no doubt that there is at least some divergence of views among the Soviet elites. Although there is not much verified information on this point, it is generally believed that there are differences in perceptions held by older as distinct from younger Soviet leaders and of military elites as contrasted with their civilian counterparts. It is also assumed that the Soviet belief system requires stricter adherence to orthodoxy on immediate issues as contrasted with longer-range problems. Finally, it is generally accepted that

---

[5] For studies of the internal politics of Soviet decisions, see Gordon Skilling and Franklin Griffiths, eds., *Interest Groups in Soviet Politics* (Princeton, N.J.: Princeton University Press, 1971); and Michael P. Gehlen, "Group Theory and the Study of Soviet Politics" in Sidney I. Ploss, ed., *Conflict and Decisionmaking in the Soviet Union* (Princeton, N.J.: Princeton University Press, 1965).

institutional affiliations affect foreign policy priorities and thus condition beliefs among the leadership.

Another qualification regarding the approach in this study is the fact that the perceptions of Soviet leaders, as is the case with non-Soviet leaders, are to some degree affected by immediate policy circumstances. While fundamental perceptions are firmly rooted in the belief system, which, in turn, is culturally derived, views of a less fundamental nature will be affected both by leadership changes in Moscow and by internal and external events. Thus less crucial perceptions are dynamic, not static, and some attitudes presented here are different from those of five years ago and doubtless will have changed five years hence.

Finally, in terms of methodological considerations, it cannot be denied that there is no infallible way of discriminating with complete confidence between true perceptions and other pronouncements. Ultimately, the analyst must make choices. For this reason, whenever there was reasonable doubt it was resolved in favor of including rather than rejecting the viewpoint in question. This approach may give somewhat more credence to the idea that the views expressed by Soviet leaders represent their true beliefs than would be concluded by a purely policy-oriented study of Soviet affairs. On the other hand, an asset of this method is the near certainty that no important Soviet statements on the subjects relevant to this book have been omitted.

Soviet Views and American Foreign Policy

Learning how to cope with an interdependent world, devising ways to reduce American dependence on oil imports, halting the spread of nuclear weapons, coexisting with China, the most populous country in the world—these are all critical problems with which America must grapple. None of these, however, is remotely comparable to the necessity to place American-Soviet relations on such a footing as to both prevent nuclear war and retain a world which is hospitable to American principles and ideals. "What to do about the Soviets" is now and has been since World War II the dominant question in U.S. national security policy; it will remain so for many years to come. It is this fact which makes it vitally necessary to understand Soviet foreign policy motivations and goals.

The reason for the criticality of superpower relations is simple: only the Soviet Union has the capability to destroy the United States, and vice versa. This shared superpower situation—total vulnerability vis-à-vis each other and virtual invulnerability vis-à-vis all other nations—has made the U.S.—USSR relationship the transcendent one in world politics. It has also brought about the belief among many influential Americans that this commonality of position, shared only by the two superpowers, could be the basis for an understanding that would usher in an era of more or less enduring peace or, at the minimum, would prevent nuclear war. Hence was born détente, a concept which implies that the mutuality of interests between Washington and Moscow transcends or at least mutes their competition. For the United States, "détente" has become the descriptive term to be applied to the Soviet-American relationship in its entirety; although the Russians occasionally speak of "détente," more often they use the phrase "peaceful coexistence."

Inevitably, the contention that the Cold War had run its course and a new, more cooperative mode of superpower interactions had begun was challenged by some Americans and ardently defended by others. Basically, three schools of thought emerged during the Nixon administration.[6] The first—officially adopted by President Nixon and his national security adviser, Dr. Henry Kissinger, and later by President Ford—could be called the "orthodox school of détente." The second school of thought—much smaller than the othodox détente group and generally containing academicians rather than policymakers—may be labeled the "revisionist détente" school. Finally a third group call themselves "realists," while their detractors call them "cold warriors."

Adherents to the orthodox détente view put forward the following propositions. First, Soviet leaders, like their American counterparts, realized that the dangers of nuclear war were such that some improvement in Soviet-American relations has become imperative.

---

[6] Dividing American opinion into only three schools of thought is an oversimplification of reality, of course, in that, among Americans who specialize in Soviet studies, there are many schools of opinion about Soviet foreign policy motivations and goals and Soviet-American relations. For a comprehensive analysis of interpretations of the USSR in world affairs by American scholars, see William Welch, *American Images of Soviet Foreign Policy* (New Haven: Yale University Press, 1970).

Specifically, détente would permit agreements to be made to limit the strategic arms race and to take other actions intended to "replace confrontation with negotiation." Reducing the risks of nuclear war was considered so central, in fact, that détente as a mode of superpower conduct is said to have begun with the signing of the SALT and other accords in Moscow in 1972.

A second Soviet motive for improving relations with the United States, according to Washington, resulted from Sino-Soviet tensions. The USSR, confronting a hostile China, naturally sought to damp down conflict with the West, to preclude the possibility (however remote) of both a two-front war and Sino-American cooperation (much more probable) directed against the Soviet Union.

A third reason why the USSR might be willing to adopt a détente policy lay in Moscow's strong desire to benefit from advanced Western technology; this could be used to induce the Soviets to be more cooperative politically. A fourth reason was closely related: the Soviet economy, particularly its agricultural sector, had severe problems which could be at least partially alleviated if the Russians could secure most-favored-nation treatment from the Americans and obtain credits which would stimulate trade between the two countries.

Finally, the orthodox détentists put forward the idea that it would be very useful to create a "web" of relationships between the Soviet Union and the United States in such nonpolitical areas as exchanges of ballet troupes and circus visits. Eventually these activities would improve the climate of superpower relations and have "spillover" effects in political spheres. "Ping-Pong diplomacy" (which acquired its name from the visit of an American table-tennis team to Peking in 1971) has been assigned a subsidiary but nevertheless important role by détente advocates. Although not an objective of détente, Ping-Pong diplomacy was one of the methods of achieving it.

These propositions, taken together, constituted a powerful argument to make détente the basis for Soviet-American relations, which was accomplished in a summit meeting in Moscow in May 1972. Altogether, the 1972 détente agreements included four groups of items.[7] The first group consisted of two arms control agreements, a five-year "interim" pact on offensive nuclear weapons and an ABM

---

[7] For the full texts of all the agreements, plus informal remarks and speeches, see Department of State, *Weekly Compilation of Presidential Documents,* VIII, No. 23 (June 5, 1972), 914-51.

treaty limiting each superpower to two ABM sites each. These military agreements institutionalized Soviet numerical superiority in numbers of ICBMs, SLBMs and aggregate "throw-weight" (total destructive missile payload capacity). Presumably, such Soviet superiorities would be at least temporarily counterbalanced by U.S. superiority in MIRVs (giving the United States a greater number of warheads) and in such qualitative areas as missile accuracy. The second part of the détente package consisted of a declaration entitled "Basic Principles of Relations Between the United States of America and the Union of Soviet Socialist Republics," which set forth the intention of the USSR and the United States to peacefully coexist and to negotiate issues rather than pursue a policy of confrontation. The third set of agreements covered many diverse "nonpolitical" subjects such as commercial relations, technological and scientific exchange, space, public health and environmental protection. The fourth group consisted of declarations of cooperative intent with regard to certain political problem areas. Specifically mentioned were a future Conference on Security and Cooperation, the status of Berlin, problems of maintaining peace in the Middle East, the Indochina conflict and the need to improve the United Nations.

Finally, in addition to these four sets of agreements, there were certain assumptions as to how the superpowers were to act toward each other and the outside world. The heart of détente is this mutual expectation of more moderate and cooperative behavior; in a relationship of nuclear parity, with "special responsibilities" devolving upon them as a result of their overwhelming world power, the two superpowers were beginning, according to détente advocates, a long process which would eventually ensure a stable and more prosperous world for all.

This does not mean that the orthodox détente school believes the détente agreements have resolved satisfactorily all differences between Soviet Russia and America. Of course there will be disagreements and certainly the two countries will be on the opposite sides of the fence on many issues. But apparently Nixon-Kissinger-Ford concluded that the Soviet Union is no longer a revolutionary power in the sense described by Dr. Kissinger himself in his book *Nuclear Weapons and Foreign Policy*. In this work, first published in 1957, Kissinger had stated that no U.S. policy could reassure the Soviet leaders about the threat America posed to the Soviet Union:

Because their doctrine *requires* them to fear us, they strive for absolute security; the neutralization of the United States and the elimination of all our influence from Europe and Asia. And because absolute security for the USSR means absolute insecurity for us, the only safe United States policy is one which is built on the assumption of a continued revolutionary struggle, even though the methods may vary with the requirements of the changing situation.[8]

That Dr. Kissinger did not casually describe the Soviet Union as a revolutionary power is evident from his frequent allusions to Soviet doctrine and the contrast between revolutionary and status quo powers, which occur in much of his writing. For example, three years after his first book, in describing asymmetries in the rival alliance systems, he wrote:

The imbalance is emphasized also by the structure of alliances in the free world as compared to the Communist bloc. The free-world alliances are composed of status quo powers. The Communist world is composed of revolutionary states of varying degrees of fanaticism.[9]

In the light of the description of Soviet Russia as a revolutionary power, opposed to the status quo, how is it that détente could be achieved, even if one granted the propositions as to why the Soviet leaders might be willing to adopt a détente stance? The answer would appear to be that President Nixon and his national security adviser no longer believed, by 1970 at least, that the USSR should be characterized as a revolutionary state. Rather, the Soviet Union was perceived as merely a great world power whose interests (naturally) collided at times with those of the other great world power, the United States. This view of the USSR was credible, however, only if the Soviets were no longer ideologically motivated, and only if Marxist-Leninist doctrine could be dismissed as mere rhetoric. The Nixon administration solved this problem by simply declaring their belief that ideology was no longer a significant factor in world politics. Thus President Nixon, in his famous "Nixon Doctrine"

---

8 Henry A. Kissinger, *Nuclear Weapons and Foreign Policy* (New York: W. W. Norton & Company, 1969 edition), p. 77. Emphasis in the original.
9 Henry A. Kissinger, *The Necessity for Choice* (New York: Harper and Brothers, 1962 edition), p. 51.

pamphlets, which annually described the Nixon-Kissinger national security policies and assumptions, referred on several occasions to the declining vitality of "isms," to the uselessness of ideology and the waning of nineteenth-century "ideological accessories of the intellectual debate." Self-interest, proclaimed the Nixon Doctrine statements, had replaced ideology. U.S. policy not only should be governed by what is in the interest of the United States; Washington would assume that all other states are likewise motivated: "It will be the policy of the United States . . . not to employ negotiations as a forum for . . . ideological debate. We will regard our Communist adversaries first and foremost as nations pursuing their own interests."[10]

The fact that Nixon and Kissinger regarded the Soviet government as only pursuing its own self-interest is in itself an unexceptional statement. What is significant is how they perceived the Soviet leaders as defining their self-interest. Although Soviet ideology was alluded to in several of the pamphlets, the thrust of the Nixon Doctrine, by logical necessity, was that the leaders of both superpowers have very similar motivations: to pursue the self-interest of their respective countries, defined in a practical way which specifically excludes revolutionary aims. If this argument by détente advocates is true, then strategic weaponry in the form of nuclear-tipped missiles, threatening unimaginable consequences should war occur, had accomplished that which countless summit meetings among political leaders and a half century of rigorous Western scholarship, which pointed out the fallacies of Marxism-Leninism, had failed to do: convert the Soviet Union from a revolutionary to a status quo power. Such a remarkable development certainly deserved most careful analysis, with at least some evidence introduced to support its plausibility. To date, however, the orthodox détente school has not addressed this problem. For this reason, détente, however desirable it may be, rests on shaky foundations.

In contrast to the orthodox détente supporters, who have controlled American foreign policy since 1969, the "revisionist détente" school and the "realists" have represented distinctly minority points of view. Revisionists, especially, have not found many prominent

---

10 Richard Nixon, *U.S. Foreign Policy for the 1970s: A New Strategy for Peace* (Washington, D.C.: U.S. Government Printing Office, 1970), p. 135.

the Soviets attach to words. Soviet writers, for example, rarely use the term "détente"; rather, they employ a phrase connoting much less friendly relations, "peaceful coexistence." Similarly, when Soviet spokesmen use words like "liberation," "freedom," "justice" and "democracy," they mean very different things from the images such words conjure up in the minds of Americans. Without at least a rudimentary understanding of Communist jargon, an outsider is completely unable to recognize the hostility frequently underlying seemingly innocent statements.

In order to clarify Moscow's political intentions, it seems appropriate to analyze what the Soviets say about themselves, the United States and the interactions of the two superpowers in world politics. This is especially important since "practical" and "hardheaded" policymakers tend to dismiss what the Soviet leaders say as "mere rhetoric" in contrast to the significance of what the Soviets do in world affairs. Again, however, this is a false dichotomy, since words really do mean something ("Bombs away!").[15] In fact, since deterrence, strategic bargaining, the political utility of force, concepts of national will and other phenomena associated with the complex nuclear balance of terror have grown in importance relative to straightforward contests of military capabilities, it can be argued that verbal policies have assumed great importance. This is so because strategic theory is at heart a psychological construct; unless the opponent is convinced that his rival has the will to use his capabilities he is not deterred from aggression. Of course, a crucial element in signaling intentions convincingly is the possession of strong forces in being; without underlying military power, retaliatory threats lack credibility. Nevertheless, verbal behavior is an essential element of strategy, since words—as well as acts—communicate to the enemy and convey to him impressions of political will. Accordingly, a correct understanding of Soviet images of the world, as evidenced by what Russian leaders say as well as what they do, has taken on an importance as yet not fully recognized. The primary objective of the chapters that follow is to provide this understanding in order to contribute to a rational American national security policy.

---

[15] This humorous illustration of the fallacy of suggesting that verbal behavior is inconsequential is from Richard Rovere, "Letter from Washington," *The New Yorker*, July 12, 1969, p. 69, as cited in Franck and Weisband, *op. cit.*, p. 118.

Soviet Images of America's Global Role

FUNDAMENTAL to an analysis of Soviet perceptions of the current U.S. global and domestic positions—and concomitant Soviet strategies in interacting with the United States—is an understanding of Soviet views on the overall global correlation of forces. Historically, the concept of a "correlation of forces" (*sootnosheniye sil*) has been applied to numerous circumstances in the domestic and international arenas. In its most general respect, the concept denotes the relative alignment of two opposing forces or groups of forces. Specifically, the correlation of world forces, which describes the relationship between capitalism and socialism, is the aggregate balance of the political, economic, military, social and scientific-technical capabilities of the two camps.

Unlike the "balance of power" concept, which the Soviets claim is derived ultimately from an evaluation of military strength even when it is used in its broadest sense, the correlation of forces concept is presented as fundamentally an estimate of class forces:

> In contrast with the concepts of bourgeois political analysts, Marxist-Leninist theory proceeds from the fact that the category of the correlation of forces in the world arena cannot and should not be reduced to the correlation of the military potential of states and that in the last analysis the correlation is none other than the *correlation*

23

of class forces on the scale of the worldwide system of international relations.[1]

Starting from this class viewpoint, Soviet analysts enumerate several elements which are examined in arriving at an overall assessment of the correlation of forces. A detailed description in the authoritative party theoretical journal *Kommunist* listed subjects under the headings of economics, military affairs, politics and international movements.[2] The economics list includes: per capita GNP; labor productivity; economic growth; level of industrial production; technical equipping of labor; labor resources and qualifications; number of specialists; level of development of theoretical and applied science. The military affairs group includes quality and quantity of armaments; firepower of armies; combat and moral qualities of soldiers; command staff training; troop organization and combat experience; character of military doctrine and thinking. The politics list includes breadth of a state's social base; mode of a state's organization of authority; possibility of making operative decisions; degree of popular support. Finally, the international movements list includes its qualitative composition; influence among the masses; position in the political life of the country; and the degree of its cohesion.

Soviet spokesmen insist that the correlation of world forces is continually shifting in favor of the socialist states led by the USSR. This thesis first emerged in the mid-1950s as part of a fundamental reassessment by the Soviet leadership of the principal trends in the international political system. These trends, in the Soviet view, warranted new interpretations of Marxism-Leninism and explained what Soviet theoreticians claimed to be the "inexorable course" of world political development:

- The transformation from a single socialist country, the USSR, to a socialist camp, encompassing Eastern Europe, China and North Korea;

- The anticolonialist movement in the developing countries—i.e., the

---

[1] A. Sergiyev, "Leninism on the Correlation of Forces as a Factor of International Relations," *Mezhdunarodnaya Zhizn'*, No. 4 (April 1975), p. 104. Emphasis in the original.

[2] G. Shakhnazarov, "On the Problem of the Correlation of Forces in the World," *Kommunist*, No. 3 (February 1974), p. 86.

national liberation struggle—regarded as a transitional stage toward socialism in the long run and as anti-Western in the short run; and

• The growing military might of the Soviet Union, reflected in the Soviet acquisition of nuclear weapons, the creation of the Warsaw Pact in 1955 and the development of intercontinental ballistic missiles beginning in 1957.

The last dimension, the military, was said to ensure the continued development of the first two: war no longer was considered "fatalistically inevitable," as Lenin had asserted. Since both the capitalist and socialist camps now had the means for unleashing considerable destruction upon each other, the capitalist states would come to realize—if they had not already—that no political purpose could be served by a war which utilized the new weapons.[3]

> The position of the aggressor under present-day conditions radically differs from his position before the Second World War. . . . In the past, wars usually ended with some capitalist countries defeating others, but the vanquished continued to live. . . . A thermonuclear war does not offer such a prospect to any aggressor, and imperialists are compelled to reckon with this.[4]

Therefore, according to Moscow, socialist and imperialist states could and must allow the principle of peaceful coexistence to govern their mutual relations, but it warned the West that the correlation of forces would continue to shift in socialism's favor, given the reduced possibilities for the imperialists to use military force to restrain the emerging socialist and national liberation movements.

It is necessary to note that in calculating the correlation of world forces, the Soviet leadership claims to look, not at isolated events, but at long-term trends, particularly those which conform to Soviet expectations concerning the "correct" and "scientifically ordained" course of world development:

> It would be very rash to draw general conclusions on the basis of individual facts, such as, for example, to assess the victory of the 1959 Cuban Revolution as a sign of absolute superiority of the

---

[3] N. S. Khrushchev, CC CPSU Accountability Report to the 20th CPSU Congress, *Pravda,* February 15, 1956.
[4] CC CPSU Letter to the Chinese, *Pravda,* April 14, 1963.

forces of socialism over imperialism, or the 1973 military-fascist coup in Chile as proof of the opposite. It is only the sum total of events taken in their dynamics that could give grounds for formulating accurate judgments on the correlation of forces in the world, and above all of the trends governing its changes.[5]

According to the Soviet position, given the "aggressive nature" of imperialism and its readiness to resort to force, or the threat to use force, in defending its interests and global position, any significant shift in Soviet-American relations required first of all a change in the military balance in favor of the Soviet Union. Only then could the immediate influence of nonmilitary factors on the correlation of forces be enhanced. While the Soviets usually argue that no single event can qualitatively change the correlation of world forces, they claim that their achievement of nuclear missile parity with the United States was the event which drastically altered the context of the East-West relationship.[6] Although Moscow began to assert that a shift had occurred in the balance of forces as early as 1956, these claims initially were based upon increasing Soviet force levels in the conventional area and were expressed somewhat tentatively. After the advent of approximate strategic parity—a condition generally assumed to have been achieved about 1969—Soviet statements became more self-confident. Comparisons between American and Soviet postures in world affairs became ever more favorable to the Russians. Furthermore, it is asserted that this new balance of power has been recognized even in the United States.

In the Soviet view, the Nixon Doctrine in 1969 and American "acquiescence" in Soviet principles of peaceful coexistence in 1972, referred to in America as "détente," were an acknowledgment by U.S. leaders that the correlation of forces had shifted in favor of the USSR.

---

[5] Shakhnazarov, *op. cit.,* p. 82.

[6] Soviet spokesmen attribute great importance to the advent of strategic parity. See G. A. Trofimenko, "Military-Strategic Aspects of the 'Nixon Doctrine,' " in Yu. P. Davydov, V. V. Zhurkin and V. S. Rudnev, eds., *Doktrina Niksona* (The Nixon Doctrine) (Moscow: "Nauka," 1972), p. 54; Marshal of the Soviet Union A. A. Grechko, USSR Minister of Defense and CC CPSU Politburo member, *Vooruzhennyye Sily Sovetskogo gosudarstva* (The Armed Forces of the Soviet State) (Moscow: Voyenizdat, 1974), p. 92.

Soviet Perceptions of the Correlation of World Forces

Strategic parity, marking the arrival of the USSR as a super-power, equal in status to the United States, is expected to bring immediate benefits to Soviet foreign policy. As Foreign Minister A. A. Gromyko expressed it, "distance cannot weaken the great attractive force of the Soviet Union's foreign policy, nor the strength, as a whole, of the ideas that our socialist state carries into the outside world."[7] This opinion was echoed by the principal leader of the Soviet Union, the Communist Party's General Secretary, L. I. Brezhnev, early in 1970 when he stated that "at the present time no question of any importance in the world can be solved without our participation, without taking into account our economic and military might."[8] Subsequent Soviet analyses of the changes in the correlation of forces between the United States and Russia consistently repeat these themes; frequently Soviet spokesmen mention 1969 as the year the USSR finally achieved equality with the United States. To determine the significance of this event, a detailed assessment of the U.S. power position was begun in 1970 by the Institute of the USA of the USSR Academy of Sciences, culminating in a major book in 1972 entitled *Doktrina Niksona*.[9] The authors state that the most significant change "to have taken place in the very structure of international relations" is:

> . . . the growing strength of the forces of socialism and their increased ability to curtail the aggressive impulses of imperialism in particular regions of the globe and, as a result, the increasing influence of the socialist countries on the development of world events and a growth in their international capacity.[10]

The result of this relative U.S. weakness, it is asserted, is the upsurge of the so-called "progressive" forces in the Third World and within the capitalist countries, as well as an intensification of the

---

[7] *Pravda,* July 11, 1969.
[8] Speech in Minsk, March 14, 1970, reported in Major General V. S. Ryabov, ed., *Dvina: The Military Maneuvers Carried Out on the Territory of Belorussia in March 1970* (Moscow: Voyenizdat, 1970), p. 8.
[9] See note 6.
[10] Pp. 8-9.

"inherent" contradictions of capitalism and the weakening of the Western alliance structure. These, in turn, affect the U.S. power position, creating a cycle from which the United States is unable to extricate itself, given the military balance between the United States and the Soviet Union.[11] It is this set of dynamics, according to Soviet analysts, which "forced" Washington to agree to the policy of peaceful coexistence or "détente" with the USSR. As a leading commentator for *Izvestiya* put it:

> I do not believe that the people who determine the foreign policy course of the United States suddenly became imbued with sympathy for the Soviet Union. It is hardly possible either to believe that the messianic visions of a Pax Americana and of the unique role which the Almighty had assigned America in the modern world have totally disappeared from them all. Imperialism remains imperialism. But times are changing and politics are changing. The leaders of world capitalism realize that it is now impossible either to intimidate or to "roll back" the Soviet Union. . . .[12]

Moreover, Soviet progress in economic development, science, technology and military capability will ensure that these changes in the Soviet-American power relationship will be irreversible. Soviet spokesmen persist in warning, however, that détente—as distinct from the correlation of forces—has not as yet been made irreversible, since despite some relative weakening, the United States still remains a formidable and dangerous opponent.

While it is apparent that Moscow perceives the United States as having failed to translate its military power into political dividends, it is equally apparent that the Soviet leadership sees itself as having converted its military capabilities into substantial political gains by attaining the ability to constrain the United States and thus acquiring for the USSR greater freedom of action in world politics. Furthermore, Soviet spokesmen describe U.S. positions in specific areas throughout the world in terms of these same dynamics, including the totality of America's global interactions, in their assessment of the correlation of world forces, with all factors overlapping and having an impact upon each other. The most significant interactions, in the Soviet view, are those involving the United States, Western Europe

---

[11] Pp. 8-27.
[12] A. Bovin, "Socialism and International Relations," *Izvestiya*, June 7, 1973.

and Japan, that is, developments within the world capitalist system; those between the United States and the countries of the Third World; and Chinese-American relations. The Soviets seem to regard the first two trends as favoring the Soviet Union while the last is seen as favoring the United States.[13]

America, Western Europe and Japan

Classical Marxist-Leninist doctrine regarded contradictions within world capitalism as inherent to the system and as the source both of inevitable class struggles within capitalist-imperialist countries and of conflicts and wars between those states. Particularly in recent years, Moscow has portrayed the West as being mired in a deepening economic, political and social crisis, "unprecedented in the history of postwar capitalism," leading to a "crumbling" of the capitalist system of controls[14] and "the disintegration of the political machinery of capitalist rule."[15] Moreover, the Soviets assert that recent events—most importantly the emergence of the USSR as a militarily strong superpower—have made impotent "the attempts of imperialism to reorganize its forces and to adjust to regional and universal changes which are occurring in the world":

> These changes are based upon the irrevocable shifting of the balance of forces in the world to the advantage of socialism and communism. The world is becoming increasingly limited in scope for the actions of capitalism and colonialism, for any kind of international adventures and artificially created crises.[16]

The conclusions the Soviet theoreticians draw from this are that "only a decisive reorganization of the entire system of international economic relations" can postpone the demise of capitalism, which is described as having reached the "twilight" of its existence.[17] Even such a "reorganization" would give only temporary respite, how-

---

13 *Doktrina Niksona*, pp. 8-10.
14 Boris Ponomarev, "The World Situation and the Revolutionary Process," *Problemy Mira i Sotsializma*, No. 6 (June 1974), pp. 6-7.
15 Brezhnev, speech delivered in Kishinev, *Pravda*, October 12, 1974.
16 Nikolay Polyanov, first deputy editor in chief of *Izvestiya*, "Inside and Outside the Alliance," *Otechestven Front* (Sofia), September 18, 1974.
17 A. Bovin, "The Twilight of Capitalism," *Krasnaya Zvezda*, October 29, 1974.

ever, since it is the objective course of history that governs the ultimate elimination of the system in any event.[18]

While certain actions undertaken by capitalist governments are
intended to ameliorate these inherent problems, Soviet analysts
acknowledge, the net effect has been a worsening of the situation.
It is asserted that although measures for capitalist economic integration—in the form of multinational corporations, economic commu-
nities such as EEC, joint industrial ventures, technology transfer and
international licensing—were undertaken to improve the capitalist
economy and improve the system of the division of labor,

> . . . integration does not eliminate the contradictions and crises,
> anarchy and disorderly development of capitalist production and
> the struggle among imperialist countries for the division of markets
> and spheres of influence, inherent in capitalism. It does not soften
> social antagonisms. All these basic vices of the capitalist system are
> reemphasized by integration, reappearing on a new scale and in
> different forms.[19]

Thus, Soviet leaders state that "the contradictions between the
United States, Western Europe and Japan continue to intensify."
Furthermore, the economic and political aspects of the crisis of the
West "are interwoven into a single skein," exacerbating relations
in all spheres and at all levels.[20] At the center of this knot of contradictions is the United States, whose position, according to Soviet
spokesmen, exemplifies the unevenness of the capitalist develop-
mental process. The role of the United States is described as "comprehensive and considerable."[21] However,

> . . . faith in U.S. omnipotence is nothing more than an illusion. For
> this reason any arguments which describe the United States as the
> potential savior of "Western civilization" are naïve and superficial,
> to say the least. . . .[22]

---

[18] M. Maksimova, head of the Department of External Economic Problems of Capi-
talism at the Institute of World Economics and International Relations (IMEMO)
USSR Academy of Sciences, *Economic Aspects of Capitalist Integration* (Moscow:
Progress Publishers, 1973), p. 332.

[19] M. Maksimova, "World Capitalist Economy and the Processes of Economic Integration," *Kommunist*, No. 16 (November 1971), p. 86.

[20] Boris Ponomarev, speech at Kremlin festivities honoring the 104th anniversary of
Lenin's birth, *Pravda*, April 23, 1974.

[21] Bovin, *op. cit.*

[22] *Ibid.*

"The real correlation of forces in the capitalist world," asserts the Director of the Institute of World Economics and International Relations, "is characterized by the relative weakening of the U.S. position, the growth of economic and financial power of Western Europe and Japan."[23] This has led to severe intercapitalist conflict featuring a competition for world markets. Ironically, it is capitalist integration, initiated in the early postwar period by the United States itself, which "objectively" created this situation. The result has been an acute "trade war" between Western Europe and Japan in one camp and the United States in the other.[24] The Soviets further contend that while the United States at the end of World War II supported the establishment of a strong Western Europe, it was aware of the risk of economic damage which could result from European integration. American leaders calculated, however, that the political and military-strategic dividends "significantly outweighed the possible losses."[25] Unfortunately for the United States, these calculations proved to be totally incorrect. The Soviet commentary concludes that the economic rivalries and concomitant political rifts between the United States and its allies "will not be easy to surmount" and are characterized by "growing pressure on the positions not only of individual U.S. monopolies but of the whole of American monopoly capital by Japan and the Western European countries."[26]

An additional source of tension between the United States and the other capitalist countries, according to Soviet observers, is the emergence of the multinational corporations, which are described as being for the most part of American origin yet not accountable to a single government. It is claimed that these "international monopolies" possess such great economic power that they have a substantial impact upon the economic development of both large and

---

23 Academician N. N. Inozemtsev, "Capitalism of the 70s: The Aggravation of Contradictions," *Pravda*, August 20, 1974.

24 Ye. N. Novosel'tsev, "The USA and Western Europe—'Mature Partnership,'" in *Doktrina Niksona*, p. 180.

25 V. F. Davydov, "The Year of Europe—A Year of Contradictions," *SShA: Ekonomika, Politika, Ideologiya* (USA: Economy, Politics, Ideology—cited hereafter as *SShA*), No. 3 (March 1974), pp. 75-76.

26 Anatoliy Gromyko and A. Kokoshin, "U.S. Foreign Policy Strategy for the 1970s," *International Affairs*, No. 10 (October 1973), pp. 69-70. Anatoliy Gromyko, the son of Soviet Foreign Minister Andrei Gromyko, is presently a Foreign Ministry official.

small states and can affect significantly the course of economic crises.[27]

The "crisis" in American economic relations with Western Europe and Japan has become a politico-military crisis, in the Soviet assessment, because those capitalist countries "which are capable of competing with the USA economically . . . have not yet found a place appropriate to their new power in the political structure of international relations."[28] These countries therefore find the subordination of their foreign policies to U.S. concerns to be less and less in their own interests as the gap between American and European power engenders a new range of contradictions between them and the United States, as has already occurred between Japan and the United States.[29] Japan is presented as an exemplar. According to Soviet analysts, these contradictions were intensified by the Nixon Doctrine, which required American allies to increase their share of the burden of defending the capitalist system against "revolutionary" encroachments without a concomitant reduction of Washington's influence either on the European continent or in Japan.[30] The overall effect of this U.S. policy, in Soviet opinion, has been to weaken the allies' faith in American willingness to protect them, while at the same time the United States continued to shape the policies of its "partners."[31]

It is within this context that the Soviets discuss NATO and the prospects for its eventual dissolution, emphasizing the current capitalist economic situation and the burden imposed upon the Western economies by defense expenditures.[32] Soviet spokesmen also assert that NATO is a vehicle for Washington's attempts to control Western European relations with the socialist bloc, claiming that the United States is trying to convince its allies that détente has been secured solely because of the American "nuclear umbrella" and troop presence in Europe.

---

[27] A. Grechikhin, chief of the Section for Capitalist Market Conditions, IMEMO, "Signs of a Profound Slump," *Izvestiya*, March 14, 1974.

[28] *Doktrina Niksona*, p. 9.

[29] *Ibid.*, pp. 9-10, 200-13.

[30] See the report of a discussion at IUSAC, "The Nixon Doctrine: Declarations and Realities," *SShA*, No. 2 (February 1971), pp. 18-48; *Doktrina Niksona*, pp. 165-83 *passim*.

[31] V. F. Davydov, *op. cit.*

[32] R. Rachkov, "Chronic Flaws," *Ekonomicheskaya Gazeta* (Economic Gazette), No. 44 (October 1974).

But such attempts have yielded very limited and contradictory results. Washington's desire to use the NATO mechanism to exercise control over "harmonization" of the approach of its West European members to development of relations with the countries of the socialist system emphasizes once again the unequal nature of relations in NATO and is tending to deepen contradictions between the United States and its allies.[33]

A salient example of the paradoxical position of the United States vis-à-vis NATO, according to Soviet spokesmen, is Washington's adoption of limited strategic options (LSO). Although former Secretary of Defense Schlesinger stated that the new strategy would broaden deterrence and guarantee the coupling of U.S. strategic forces with the security of Western Europe, the Soviet interpretation is that the LSO "fundamentally contradicts the peoples' vital interests and the interests of further relaxing tension on the European continent."[34] Furthermore, the Soviets contend that the LSO doctrine is merely a new form of the Kennedy-era Defense Department's "city-avoidance" theory, intended to save American population centers at the expense of European cities.[35] Acceptance of the concept of "extended deterrence" through LSO demonstrates "the readiness of the NATO allies to throw themselves into the fire of a nuclear war."[36]

Russian analysis of NATO, consequently, is that political, economic and military factors are increasingly separating the European side of the alliance from the American. The United States is unable to devise formulas for offsetting the rift and American attempts to do so have merely exacerbated the relationship. In addition, leftist successes along NATO's southern flank[37] and the broadening of Soviet relations with NATO members are said to be further indications of the alliance's hastening collapse:

It is not accidental that the North Atlantic bloc has turned out to

---

33 V. S. Shein, "USA-NATO-EEC," *SShA*, No. 8 (August 1974), p. 44.
34 Captain 1st Rank V. Pustov and Captain Yu. Gavrilov, "Détente or 'Deterrent'?" *Krasnaya Zvezda*, March 10, 1974.
35 M. A. Mil'shteyn and L. S. Semeyko, "The Problem of the Inadmissibility of a Nuclear Conflict (On New Approaches in the USA)," *SShA*, No. 11 (November 1974), p. 11.
36 Yu. Yakhontov, *Pravda* commentator, Radio Moscow, February 4, 1974.
37 For a detailed Soviet analysis of leftist movements in Europe, see B. N. Ponomarev, speech at meeting of All-Army Conference of Ideological Workers, *Krasnaya Zvezda*, January 29, 1975.

be facing an actual crisis. The NATO flanks are crumbling. In the headquarters of the bloc they are frantically searching for "replacement" partners in connection with the growing anti-NATO sentiments in Greece, Portugal and Turkey.[38]

It must be noted in this regard that while this course of events in Europe is considered propitious from the Soviet standpoint, optimism is tempered by caution; Moscow has become alarmed over what it perceives as a growing threat of "neo-fascism" in such countries as Portugal, West Germany and Italy. While Soviet spokesmen claim that fascism is an endemic outgrowth of capitalism-imperialism, they regard its appearance as more likely during periods of socioeconomic instability and warn that "in the nuclear age the strengthening of fascism and, even more, the fascist seizure of state power, would be even more dangerous for mankind than on the eve of World War II."[39] Although Moscow might perceive new opportunities for weakening the Western alliance system and for a growing "Finlandization" of Western Europe, therefore, future developments cannot be predicted with confidence; "it would be wrong to regard them as some automatic process developing without obstacles."[40]

The Soviets describe the U.S. position vis-à-vis Japan as essentially similar to American-Western European relations, since "inherent" contradictions are present in all intercapitalist economic, political and military interactive processes, regardless of region.

> Thus the relations of the USA and Japan as a whole in the current phase are characterized by a complex interweaving of cooperation engendered by common imperialist interests and a conflict whose outlines are becoming increasingly perceptible. This last trend should not, of course, be overevaluated. Japan is still strongly dependent on the USA in economic, political and military terms. The ruling circles of the USA are convinced that they will be able to keep Japan as an American partner.[41]

The American-Japanese alliance is said to be characterized by a

---

[38] T. Kolesnichenko, "International Review," *Pravda*, March 30, 1975.

[39] Ponomarev, *Krasnaya Zvezda*, January 29, 1975.

[40] D. Tomashevskiy, "Toward a Radical Restructuring of International Relations," *Mirovaya Ekonomika i Mezhdunarodnyye Otnosheniya* (World Economics and International Relations), No. 1 (January 1975), p. 9.

[41] G. A. Orionova, "Japan—Rival or Partner?" in *Doktrina Niksona*, p. 213.

"crisis of confidence" caused by currency and trade problems between the two countries. The economic problems in the relationship, according to Soviet analysis, "directly affect a subject of long-standing dispute in American-Japanese relations, which is the U.S. demand for Japan to increase its contribution to the 'mutual defense' system."[42] The net result is an atmosphere of tension and mistrust, permeating all areas of Japanese-American relations.[43] The United States, it is claimed, wants to "push" Japan into remaining a "junior" partner in carrying out Washington's policies in Asia, but fears that Japan might become too strong militarily, thus "reincarnating" the factors which existed in the 1930s.[44]

According to Soviet accounts, the 1973-74 oil embargo and the resultant energy crisis graphically illustrated the growing contradictions between the United States and its allies. Soviet spokesmen assert that "the foundations of the energy crisis are laid by the very system of the capitalist economy," since capitalism prevents the rational and balanced use of raw material resources in all sectors of society and capitalist countries obstruct the equitable division of labor between themselves and the developing countries.[45] The oil crisis, moreover, is claimed to be the "turning point" in the rift between the United States and Western Europe-Japan, because it was the catalyst in converting latent hostilities into tangible foreign policies. Most notable in this respect, according to Soviet spokesmen, were the "independent" course pursued by Western Europe and Japan during and after the October War and the NATO allies' acute displeasure over Washington's use of bases on their territories to aid Israel "without consulting them."[46]

> The world is witnessing a sharp exacerbation of contradictions—economic, political and military—between the United States of America and Western European NATO allies. To the discontent of the latter over Washington's unilateral actions during the military conflict in the Middle East in October 1973 have been added

---

[42] G. A. Orionova, "A 'Crisis of Confidence' in American-Japanese Relations," *SShA*, No. 11 (November 1973), p. 42.

[43] See V. A. Kremenyuk, "Regional Trends in the Foreign Policy of the USA," *SShA*, No. 5 (May 1975), pp. 47-49.

[44] Orionova, in *Doktrina Niksona*, pp. 202-03.

[45] Inozemtsev, *op. cit.*

[46] Yu. Goloshubov, "Big and Little Europe," *Izvestiya*, December 14, 1973.

sharp differences over the ways for overcoming the energy crisis and over the policy toward countries of the Arab East.[47]

In addition, Moscow has portrayed Washington as attempting to use the oil monopolies—which, they point out, are based in the United States—to curtail Europe's oil supplies as a means to ameliorate the U.S. energy crisis. Consequently, the Soviets conclude that Western solidarity, "especially when it is a question of economic interest, is an entirely ephemeral thing."[48] The oil crisis, in their expressed view, is evidence of the worthlessness of U.S. hopes and promises for a commonality of interests in the Western World and underlines the necessity for America's allies to decouple their interests from the global policies of the United States. This is feasible now that peaceful coexistence is a fact of life in Soviet relations with all capitalist countries.

America and the Third World

An integral factor in the dynamics of the correlation of world forces, in the Soviet estimation, is the transformation occurring in the developing countries of Asia, Africa and Latin America, particularly the "strengthening of their independence" from the capitalist countries and especially the United States:

> Having at their disposal considerable material and manpower resources, the developing countries are exerting a growing influence on international affairs.[49]

The socialist countries, however, are credited with playing a decisive role in this process of national liberation; the successes of the national liberation movement "would have been impossible without the existence of the Soviet Union and without the tremendous and irreplaceable political, moral and material support which it gives the peoples fighting imperialism."[50]

---

[47] A. Antonov, "NATO and Détente," *Soviet Military Review*, No. 6 (June 1974), p. 56.
[48] Yu. Danov, "Waking Up One Day," *Sotsialisticheskaya Industriya* (Socialist Industry), November 13, 1973.
[49] Shakhnazarov, *op. cit.*, p. 80.
[50] B. N. Ponomarev, "Topical Problems in the Theory of the World Revolutionary Process," *Kommunist*, No. 15 (October 1971), p. 65.

The key factor in guaranteeing the forward development of the revolutionary struggles said to be occurring within all Third World countries and with regard to their foreign policies, in the Soviet assessment, is the attainment by the USSR of strategic parity, which imposes a restraint upon the United States:

> . . . this could not happen while the imperialist countries retained overwhelming military superiority, used unhesitatingly to resolve in their favor international conflicts and to suppress the national liberation struggle of oppressed peoples. . . . Only the fact of losing absolute military superiority and realizing the limit beyond which the use of military force would no longer lead to the achievement of age-old political objectives, but could mean suicide, led the ruling circles of the capitalist countries to begin to understand the inevitability of peaceful coexistence.[51]

It is essential to note in this regard that peaceful coexistence, as "codified" in the U.S.-Soviet agreement signed in 1972 in Moscow, is defined by Russian leaders as a renunciation only of war between the great powers; it in no way signifies a rejection of Soviet abetment of and assistance to revolutionary violence in the form of wars of national liberation.[52]

Moscow's formulation regarding wars of liberation and the desired extent of Soviet involvement has evolved from the Khrushchevian emphasis on "peaceful roads to socialism"—a corollary to the doctrine of noninevitability of war—and "victory through competition" to the current concept of the acceptability of violence in Third World areas. Khrushchev initially had appeared to oppose all local wars, including wars of liberation. In 1960, however, in the aftermath of Chinese criticism that the USSR was subordinating world revolutionary interests to Soviet relations with the West, the Soviet leader insisted that he had never intended to allow the general line of peaceful coexistence to modify support for Third World conflicts. Nonetheless, the basic thrust of the Khrushchevian approach was that local wars, whatever their source, should be discouraged, al-

---

51 Shakhnazarov, *op. cit.*, p. 80. See also CC CPSU Theses for Lenin Birth Centenary, *Pravda*, December 23, 1969; L. I. Brezhnev, speech in Moscow, June 5, 1972, *Pravda*, June 6, 1972; N. N. Inozemtsev, "Lenin's Theory of Imperialism and the Present," *Kommunist*, No. 6 (April 1974), p. 66.
52 A. N. Kosygin, speech at a reception in Moscow for Fidel Castro, *Pravda*, July 4, 1972.

though Soviet views on this were ambiguous and policy was inconsistent and opportunistic.[53] A definitive Soviet line regarding violence did not arise until the advent of the current leadership. It is
apparent that this change in emphasis after Khrushchev was based
largely upon a perception of the gradually eroding willingness of the
United States to intervene in national liberation conflicts. As Soviet
military power increased, and a condition of strategic parity was
attained, Soviet confidence rose and Moscow clearly began to believe that the United States would henceforth have to assume a more
passive posture vis-à-vis the Third World. Thus, the deputy head of
the International Department of the Central Committee of the Communist Party of the Soviet Union wrote in 1972:

> In the course of competition between two opposing social systems,
> the chances increase for socialism to render support to the revolu-
> tionary and liberation movement in the nonsocialist part of the
> world. Economic successes facilitate a growth in the defensive
> might of countries of socialism. . . . The defensive might of the
> Soviet Union was and is the chief obstacle on the path of imperial-
> ist warmongers.[54]

Similarly, according to the Director of the Main Political Administration of the Soviet Army and Navy:

> One cannot fail to see that the military might of the socialist com-
> munity serves as an obstacle to the export of counterrevolution by
> the imperialists and thus *objectively promotes the development of
> revolutionary and liberation movements.*[55]

Moscow now asserts that American "hegemony" over the Third
World has declined significantly. "The graveyard of Vietnam"[56]
is presented as the most acute and trying of the many failures the
United States is claimed to have suffered in its role as "guarantor and
protector of the international system of exploitation and oppres-

---

[53] For discussion of this, see Stephen P. Gibert, "Wars of Liberation and Soviet Military Aid Policy," *Orbis*, Fall 1966, pp. 841-44.

[54] V. V. Zagladin, ed., *Mezhdunarodnoye Kommunisticheskoye Dvizheniye: Ocherk
Strategii i Taktiki* (The International Communist Movement: Sketch of Strategy
and Tactics), JPRS No. 57044-1 (Moscow: Politizdat, 1972), p. 57.

[55] General of the Army A. A. Yepishev, "The Soviet Army's Historic Mission," *Soviet
Military Review*, No. 2 (February 1974), p. 6. Emphasis in the original.

[56] A. A. Grechko, speech at 24th CPSU Congress, *Pravda*, April 4, 1971.

sion."[57] The U.S. leadership has learned a lesson, in the Soviet view. Washington's acceptance of the principles of peaceful coexistence and American recognition of the change in the correlation of world forces is the most striking demonstration of this lesson: "War is no longer suitable as a means of resolving disputes between states" and thus "aggressive imperialist wars lose their point because of their obvious futility (the outcome of the U.S. war in Vietnam is proof of this)."[58] In addition, actions taken by "progressive" forces in the Third World in the period of peaceful coexistence are said in general to advance Soviet interests and thus to contribute to the growing shift in the correlation of world forces. The Soviets argue that trends in what are viewed as U.S. "vital" regions indicate that the American position will continue to weaken. With regard to Latin America, for example, it is asserted:

> Seemingly quite reliable rear areas of American imperialism are becoming a tremendous hotbed of anti-imperialist revolution. A tremendously powerful revolutionary movement is developing by the side of the main citadel of imperialism, the United States.[59]

The impact of the decline in the U.S. position vis-à-vis the developing countries—and particularly those in Latain America and the Middle East—impinges upon Washington's relations with its own allies, as well as with the Third World states in question, due to the network of economic linkages between the capitalist and developing worlds. Soviet spokesmen characterize Third World actions against capitalism—including expropriations of foreign concessions, price increases on raw materials and the creation of export associations—as liberationist and as furthering significantly the world struggle against imperialism. In this struggle, it is anticipated that the Soviet Union will play an increasingly important role. One writer invoked Leninist authority to point out:

> Victorious in one country, the proletariat must not only defend its

---

[57] Brezhnev, report to 24th CPSU Congress, *Pravda,* March 31, 1971.

[58] V. Osipov, *Izvestiya* observer, "Détente and Nothing Else," *Novoye Vremya* (New Times), No. 7 (February 15, 1974), pp. 8-9.

[59] Ponomarev, "Topical Problems in the Theory of the World Revolutionary Process," p. 62. See also A. Aleksin, "The 'Quiet' Intervention," *Kommunist*, No. 10 (July 1970), p. 92; A. A. Atroshenko, "The Principle of a 'New Partnership' for the Western Hemisphere," in *Doktrina Niksona*, pp. 214-21.

own socialist achievements, but also give direct assistance, including military assistance, to the proletarian revolutionary movement in other countries. This is, taught V. I. Lenin, one of its most important international tasks. Military support could be carried out by various means and methods: by sending detachments, military advisers, specialists, by supplying weapons, ammunition, etc.[60]

According to the Soviet view, such assistance is not seen as being in contradiction with the policies of peaceful coexistence and détente; these policies apply solely to relations between the capitalist and socialist countries and expressly exclude the Third World. Thus, for example, military aid to the North Vietnamese and Viet Cong was not viewed as inconsistent with peaceful coexistence.

> For many years, the Soviet Union gave effective support and vast unselfish assistance to the Vietnamese people in strengthening their defense and in their struggle against aggression. . . . This is one illustration of how closely the two basic principal lines of USSR foreign policy are entwined—the policy of peaceful coexistence with capitalist states and the policy of rendering assistance and support to progressive, anti-imperialist forces. . . .[61]

The developing countries are credited with having contributed to the disruption of the Western alliance and in particular with having counterposed the United States against its allies. The result has been the exacerbation of "inherent" capitalist contradictions and the attainment of a new stage in the development of the national liberation struggle. This new phase, according to Soviet analysts, is a struggle for economic independence from capitalism, as a necessary sequel to the political independence achieved by anticolonial forces in the postwar period:

> Having strengthened their political independence in the protracted struggle against imperialism, the developing countries launched a powerful offensive against the entire system of their exploitation in the world capitalist economy under conditions of growing raw materials and fuel shortage at the beginning of the seventies. They are making use of the enormous dependence of the industrial cen-

---

[60] Colonel (Reserves) M. Molodtsygin, "Leninist Principle of Internationalism in the Organization of the Military Defense of Socialist Countries," *Voyenno-Istoricheskiy Zhurnal* (Military-History Journal), No. 9 (September 1974), p. 4.

[61] "Recommendations for Seminar Lessons," *Kommunist Vooruzhennykh Sil*, No. 21 (November 1973), p. 21.

ters of capitalism on reserves and supplies from the developing countries of such important types of mineral raw materials as oil, tin, manganese, bauxite, cobalt, diamonds and rare elements.[62]

Of particular significance in this regard is the impact of the West's growing sensitivity to and dependence upon petroleum imported from the Third World, especially from the Middle East. In June 1973, prior to the oil crisis generated by the October War, *Pravda* noted that "to stop pumping Arabian Gulf oil in the present situation will be like an economic earthquake to the entire capitalist economy."[63] In addition to causing rifts between the United States and its allies, Soviet leaders say, the oil problem has forced the United States "to maneuver in the Arab world."[64] Furthermore, the standard Soviet formulation that "no interests of the development of interstate relations with capitalist countries have ever been able to make the USSR depart . . . [from] positions of solidarity with and assistance to other detachments of the revolutionary movement"[65] is claimed to apply in the Middle East in the era of Soviet-American détente. The Soviets state that the practice of peaceful coexistence will not soften their support for the use of the "oil weapon" by the Arabs against the West, since the Soviet Union "does not intend to develop its economic relations with the United States at the expense of the interests of the Arab states."[66]

Soviet officials thus not only affirmed their approval but actively encouraged such actions on the part of the Arab states as the 1972 nationalization of the Iraq Petroleum Company by the Baghdad regime[67] and the 1973-74 oil embargo and price increase by the oil-producing countries in the wake of the October War.[68] The suc-

---

[62] R. Andreasyan, senior researcher in IMEMO, "The Problems of Raw Materials," *Pravda,* April 1, 1975.

[63] A. Vasil'yev, "Oil and Politics," *Pravda,* June 10, 1973.

[64] Ye. M. Primakov, deputy director of IMEMO, commenting on Radio Moscow Domestic Service, August 19, 1973; also Primakov, "U.S. Maneuvers in the Middle East," *Pravda,* June 5, 1971.

[65] B. N. Ponomarev, "V. I. Lenin—The Great Leader of the Revolutionary Era," *Kommunist,* No. 18 (December 1969), p. 18.

[66] R. Andreasyan, report over Radio Moscow International Service, September 12, 1973.

[67] See, for instance, V. Kudryavtsev, "Iraq on Its Way," *Izvestiya,* June 7, 1972.

[68] B. Rachkov, "Oil and the Monopolies' Maneuvers," *Ekonomicheskaya Gazeta,* No. 14 (April 1974). For discussion of this, see Foy Kohler, Leon Goure and Mose Harvey, *The Soviet Union and the October 1973 Middle East War* (Miami, Fla.: University of Miami Press, 1974), especially Ch. 6.

cess of the Arab countries in gaining increasing control over their oil and in turning it against their former "exploiters" has been attributed to the "general weakening of the West and the shift in the East-West correlation of forces," as well as to the "cooperation between the Arab countries and the Soviet Union" in the era of Soviet-American détente, which made it more difficult "for the monopolies to pursue their policy of exploitation" in the Third World.[69] The stated Soviet view is that closer relations with the Soviet Union are essential for any Third World producer countries if they are to defend themselves against the United States, which will attempt in one form or another to regain its former control over these countries and their natural resources.[70] Within the context of this struggle, the Soviets portray Israel as the main regional surrogate of American imperialism in the Middle East and include the Arab countries among those struggling for global liberation:

> The Soviet Union regards the Middle East [i.e., Arab-Israeli] crisis not as a clash of national interests but as an attempt by world imperialism with the aid of the Israeli elite—which is pursuing its own expansionist aims here—to strike a blow against the national liberation movement in the Arab countries.[71]

Despite the defeats suffered by the United States in its relations with the Third World and the optimism expressed in Soviet commentaries on the prospects of further deterioration in these relations, Soviet analysts concede that the course of events in the developing countries is complex and often contradictory. They warn that the majority of the young states "remain within the world capitalist system," and that one should not "assume that imperialism has exhausted its possibilities in the area of control over the young national states."[72] It is recognized that although many of the developing countries that export raw materials have gained considerable eco-

---

[69] R. Andreasyan, "Middle East: The Oil Factor," *New Times*, No. 45-46 (November 1973), p. 19; see also Brezhnev's speech in Moscow at the dinner honoring Tito of Yugoslavia, *Pravda*, November 13, 1973, and his speech before the Indian Parliament in New Delhi, *Pravda*, November 30, 1973.

[70] V. Mayevskiy, "Oil and the 'Third World,' " *Pravda*, April 3, 1974.

[71] Ye. M. Primakov, "The Path Toward a Just Peace," *Pravda*, October 15, 1970; also Brezhnev, speech to the Indian Parliament, cited above.

[72] Ye. Tarabin, "The 'Third World' and Imperialism: A New Alignment of Forces," *Mirovaya Ekonomika i Mezhdunarodnyye Otnosheniya*, No. 2 (February 1975), pp. 13, 16.

nomic and political leverage, they tend to look to the West as their principal trade market, source of technology and area of investment for surplus funds.

Nevertheless, Soviet spokesmen contend that American recognition of the change in the correlation of world forces, which culminated in the détente relationship, must be followed by a realization in Washington that U.S. policies toward the developing countries had better change, in order to conform with diminished American capabilities and opportunities in the Third World regions:

> This is linked with the assessments of the raw material, fuel and power problems faced by the USA and other leading capitalist states for the last decade of the century. These estimates indicate that in coming years the USA will be much more dependent on the sources of raw materials in the developing countries and on the eventuality that these countries will raise the price of raw materials (as has already been done in the case of oil). This makes it imperative for the USA to adopt serious political decisions today.[73]

Consequently, according to the Russian interpretation, since neither the "positions of strength" (interventionist) policies nor application of the "partnership" (Nixon Doctrine) concept can work under present conditions, the United States is obliged to conduct its affairs in the Third World in accordance with the norms of the principles of peaceful coexistence, as defined by the Soviet Union.

Assessments of Sino-Soviet American Interactions

While the Soviets describe the correlation of world forces as having shifted in their favor and expect further development in that direction as an "objective, law-governed process," this assessment is complicated by the "Chinese factor."[74] The foreign and domestic policies of the leadership of the People's Republic of China since the late 1950s have caused "to a significant degree certain difficulties and complications in the development of the world system of socialism

---

[73] L. I. Brezhnev, speech before the World Peace Congress in Moscow, *Pravda*, October 26, 1973; Ponomarev, "The Role of Socialism in Modern World Development," *op. cit.*

[74] G. A. Trofimenko, "Some Aspects of U.S. Military and Political Strategy," *SShA*, No. 10, JPRS 51895 (October 1970), p. 19.

and the anti-imperialist movement." According to Soviet analysts, this was brought about by the Maoist ruling group's divergence from the "correct path" of Marxism-Leninism to the "dangerous path" of "Sinocentrism":

> Breaking with scientific socialism, the Maoists took the path of enmity in respect to the USSR and the other socialist countries and struggled against the international communist and workers' movement and against the cohesion of all revolutionary and liberation forces, sliding to positions where they were actually rubbing shoulders with the most reactionary, aggressive circles of imperialism.[75]

In the open communications which formally heralded the Sino-Soviet rift, the Soviet leaders accused their Chinese counterparts of attempting to undermine the peaceful coexistence relationship between East and West, thus obstructing the development of the world revolutionary movement, which could progress more easily behind the shield of peaceful coexistence.[76] Although Chinese foreign policy subsequent to the Cultural Revolution was markedly different from that of the early 1960s, which, together with a change in U.S. foreign policy, culminated in a limited Sino-American rapprochement, the substance of the Soviet attack has not changed but has been adapted to the current conditions of Sino-Soviet-U.S. interactions and to the Soviet assessment of the changed power relationship between the United States and the Soviet Union. While in the 1960s the Soviets argued that the Chinese were attempting to subvert Soviet principles of peaceful coexistence by being openly hostile toward the West and advocating war to further communism, recent events have led Soviet spokesmen to conclude that the Soviet Union is now viewed by the Chinese as a greater enemy than the West. Accordingly, Soviet analysts claim that Chinese attempts at normalizing relations with the United States are aimed at destroying U.S.-Soviet détente.[77] Similarly, the Chinese "anti-Sovietism" of today, in the Soviet view, is directed against "all the progressive forces" in the world.[78] It is therefore apparent that the Soviet leadership,

---

[75] I. Aleksandrov, "Slogans and Practice," *Pravda*, February 5, 1975.

[76] *Pravda*, April 14, 1963, and July 14, 1963.

[77] B. N. Zanegin, "On Certain Aspects of American-Chinese Relations," *SShA*, No. 2 (February 1975), p. 34.

[78] A. G. Kruchinin, "Peking's Struggle Against the Socialist Community," *Problemy Dal'nego Vostoka* (Problems of the Far East), No. 1 (January 1974), p. 33.

throughout the fifteen or so years of institutionalized and formalized Sino-Soviet hostility, has managed to fit changing Chinese modes of behavior into an unchanged Soviet perceptual framework of hostility toward Peking. Transformations which have occurred in China's foreign policy (and in the foreign policy of the United States) in the past five years, coinciding with a Soviet calculation of a definitive, irreversible change in the overall balance of power brought about by the advent of Soviet-American strategic parity, have failed to alter the Soviets' overall characterization of China as their prime "enemy" and "betrayer."

Although, on the one hand, the PRC's estrangement from the Soviet bloc is regarded by Moscow as a setback for the "forces of progress," the Sino-American normalization of relations is portrayed, on the other hand, as a manifestation of the extent to which the correlation of forces already has shifted:

> . . . this normalization itself became possible as a result both of the radical change in the correlation of forces in the world arena in favor of socialism, peace and progress, and of the consistent and principled struggle of the socialist countries for the relaxation of international tension. These successes led to the failure of the gamble on "containing" communism which, for almost a quarter of a century, had lain at the foundation of United States foreign policy toward the socialist countries, including the PRC.[79]

Nevertheless, it is claimed that trends exist in Washington's foreign policy which are inconsistent with the international relaxation of tension. America's attempt at making China a "structural element in the 'balance of power' system"—that is, a counterweight to the USSR—is portrayed as evidence of Washington's continued adherence to an antagonistic policy toward the Soviet Union.[80]

Soviet spokesmen contend that American exacerbation of Sino-Soviet hostility is a consequence of Washington's adoption of a "triangular" foreign policy. According to Soviet analysts, the situation in Asia changed in the late 1960s, due primarily to America's inability to continue its militarist course. "The economic rebirth of Japan, the stabilization of India as an independent state, and the increased role of a number of other states in this region" created a

---

[79] Zanegin, *op. cit.*, p. 33.
[80] *Ibid.*, p. 35.

"vacuum" which the United States has intended to fill by promoting Chinese influence on the Asian continent.[81]

> The first signs of a thaw in the American attitude toward China were detected in the summer of 1969 and coincided fully in time with proclamation of the Guam [i.e., Nixon] Doctrine.[82]

In sum, the general Soviet appraisal of the "Chinese factor" is that the United States, recognizing the changed correlation of forces, has sought to compensate for it through overtures to China, thus restoring the world balance of power to American advantage.

Foreign Policy Implications

The salient Soviet perception concerning the global role of the United States, a perception which to a greater or lesser degree affects all other Soviet images of the United States, is that the world correlation of forces is shifting inexorably in favor of the USSR. In its larger dimension this describes the Soviet view of the confrontation between the two major world systems, socialism versus capitalism. On this plane the Soviets also see the aggregate balance tending toward the eventual supremacy of the socialist camp. In assessing the impact of this perception, it is important to note two factors which affect the firmness of its position in Soviet thought: first, the Soviets look at long-term trends, and are not distracted by isolated events which by themselves might constitute a setback for their side; and second, the trend perceived is in accord with the Soviet conception of the "scientifically ordained" course of world history. Thus conditioned by the intangibles of ideology and self-image and by the observable concrete phenomena which in Soviet eyes appear to confirm their expectations, this attitude is unlikely to be shaken. Although Soviet theory holds that no single event can significantly alter the basic trend in the correlation of forces, they do regard one development to be of such importance that it transcends the general rule; this event was the achievement of strategic nuclear parity with

---

[81] V. P. Lukin, "American-Chinese Relations: Concepts and Reality," *SShA*, No. 2 (February 1973), pp. 16-19; M. V. Senina, "The 'Nixon Doctrine' and the 'Chinese Factor,'" in *Doktrina Niksona*, p. 141.
[82] Senina, *op. cit.*, p. 142.

the United States, which occurred about the year 1969. Soviet attitudes, declarations and actions became noticeably more bold after that time. The Soviets believe that as a consequence of the arrival of the historic milestone of strategic parity, the United States and the West were forced to accept détente, or peaceful coexistence, as the basis for Soviet-American relationships and as a general guideline for capitalism's interactions with socialism. The ending of American military superiority, the intensification of the contradictions of capitalism and the erosion of Western alliance structures have in the Soviet view combined to place the United States in a cycle from which it cannot extricate itself. Détente was, therefore, America's only option.

The impact of this key Soviet perception regarding the correlation of forces is, if unchanged, adverse to U.S. interests. Its generally unfavorable impact extends to the other three major domains of U.S. global interactions discussed in this chapter—that is, with respect to the U.S.-Western Europe-Japan arena, to U.S.-Third World relations, and to U.S.-PRC-USSR relationships. To generalize about Soviet perceptions of the United States in these four domains: the impact in the area of Soviet-American interactions is generally adverse; in the U.S.-Western Europe-Japan arena and in American-Third World relations it is mixed in impact; and in the fourth, the U.S.-PRC-USSR triangle, it is somewhat more positive for American foreign policy than negative.

If one were to identify a single critical Soviet perception which more than any other represents a counterbalance to the view of the correlation of forces, it would be that the Soviet Union tempers its basic belief that capitalism is doomed with the pragmatic recognition that the end is not yet in sight. That is, the United States and the West will continue to constitute a formidable obstacle to the freedom of the Soviet Union and the socialist camp to expand their global reach. A still vital capitalist world will be able to defend itself, to protect its interests in critical world zones of confrontation and to act intelligently and capably in coping with the challenges of an increasingly interdependent world. The essential ingredient to realize the positive potential of the Soviet perception that capitalism is not yet dead is intangible: the will to compete, to stay the long course of intersystemic competition. The present Soviet perception is that America's will to resist what the Soviets see as an ongoing shift in power and influence in their favor is eroding. Thus the broad challenge imposed by the aggregate of Soviet perceptions of the United States is not whether the United States has the capability to compete but whether it can sustain its moral force for survival and effectively communicate this, in both word and deed, to the men in Moscow.

The United States
through Soviet Eyes

Soviet officials, in endeavoring to understand and explain American policies and activities in the foreign policy arena, in recent years have made a considerable effort to study the internal political, economic, social and ideological factors operating in the United States, which they perceive to be interdependent with the international environment. The Soviet world outlook proceeds from a "class" perspective—that is, it prescribes an analysis of phenomena in terms of bourgeois-proletarian and capitalist-socialist dichotomies. Strengths and vulnerabilities are interpreted through an explanation of the "objective reality," a condition of which is the dynamic interdependence of internal and external forces. In order to demonstrate the interdependence between domestic and global factors and their relevance to the changes which have occurred in the correlation of world forces, Soviet analysts assert:

> As long ago as the beginning of the seventies, past experience made the U.S. ruling circles abandon their unsuccessful attempts to resolve urgent domestic problems by all kinds of international adventures and an unrestrained arms race. In recent years the understanding has grown in responsible U.S. spheres that one cannot even embark on the practical resolution of domestic problems without a favorable atmosphere in the world arena. This is why the significance of foreign policy questions is now being emphasized with special force.[1]

---

[1] V. M. Berezhkov, "The Only Alternative," *SShA*, No. 9 (September 1974), p. 3; Berezhkov is chief editor of *SShA*.

The United States and the General Crisis of Capitalism

According to Soviet analysts, the post-World War I international situation gave rise to a "general crisis of capitalism" (*obshchiy krizis kapitalizma*), which is described as "the historic period during which occurs the process of the revolutionary downfall of capitalism and its replacement by socialism on a worldwide scale."[2] In the main speech to the 24th CPSU Congress in 1971, Brezhnev asserted that "the general crisis of capitalism continues to deepen" despite capitalism's attempts to adapt to the changing international situation.[3] Quoting himself on this point at the 25th Congress in 1976, Brezhnev stated further that "the events of recent years with new force confirm that capitalism is a society devoid of a future."[4] Thus, the factors which lead to the exacerbation of the general crisis of capitalism are viewed as significantly contributing to the shift in the correlation of forces in favor of socialism.

By commonly accepted Soviet standards, the general crisis of capitalism is divided into three broad stages,[5] whose periodization is derived from "the essential change of the correlation of forces between capitalism and socialism."[6] The first stage began with the emergence of the first socialist state after World War I and lasted until the beginning of World War II. Within this stage are chronicalized three specific crises corresponding to the years 1920-21, 1929-33, 1937-38. The second stage arose as a consequence of the defeat of fascist Germany and the emergence of several socialist states and lasted into the

2 I. T. Rogovsky, *Politicheskaya ekonomiya kapitalizma* (The Political Economy of Capitalism) (Minsk: Publishing House of Belorussian State University *imeni* V. I. Lenin, 1975), p. 228.

3 L. I. Brezhnev, "Accountability Report of the Central Committee of the CPSU to the 24th Congress of the Communist Party of the Soviet Union," in *XXIV s"yezd Kommunisticheskoy partii Sovetskogo Soyuza. Stenograficheskiy otchet*, Vol. I (Moscow: Politizdat, 1971), p. 38. Italicized in the original.

4 *Pravda*, February 25, 1976.

5 For several recent discussions of the periodization of the general crisis of capitalism, see, for example, Rogovskiy, *op. cit.*, pp. 228-32, and I. Gur'yev, "The General Crisis of Capitalism and Its Further Deepening," *Mirovaya Ekonomika i Mezhdunarodnyye Otnosheniya*, No. 10 (October 1975), pp. 34-36.

6 "The General Crisis of Capitalism" in *Bolshaya Sovetskaya Entsiklopediya* (The Great Soviet Encyclopedia), Vol. XVIII (Moscow: Publishing House of the Soviet Encyclopedia, 1974), p. 252.

mid-1950s. During this time occurred the specific crises of 1948-49 and 1953-54. The third, and present, stage is dated as of the mid-1950s. As one Soviet source noted:

> Deep qualitative changes took place in the socialist system in the mid-50s. The socialist people started the full-scale construction of communist society. The multi-layered structure of the economy was on the whole liquidated in a majority of the countries of people's democracy, and they entered into the concluding stage of the construction of socialism. Under the leadership of the Leninist Communist Party, the Soviet people created mighty missile and space equipment, laid the foundation of the approaching space triumphs—the first artificial satellites in the world, the historic flight of Yu. A. Gagarin, the first ground launching into outer space. The successes of the socialist economy and Soviet science permitted the creation of powerful means of defense, which forever excluded the possibility of the restoration of the aggressive capitalist path.
>
> Put together in the international arena, all of these altered the correlation of forces of the two systems in favor of socialism. As a result, after the second half of the 50s arose a new, third stage of the deepening of the general crisis of capitalism.[7]

Within the third stage are delineated crises occurring in 1957-58, 1960-61, 1969-70 and 1973 to the present.

In a report to the second joint scientific conference of IUSAC and IMEMO, held in July 1975, one speaker noted that the 1973-75 capitalist crisis has been "the deepest and most severe crisis since the beginning of the 1930s" and that it marks "a definite landmark in the development of the general crisis of capitalism."[8] A second speaker at the conference supported this position, noting that "in all its 'parameters'—in duration, scale and severity, and in the problems generated by it—the present crisis is the most severe of all the crises in the postwar history of the USA."[9] Among the major elements of the present crisis are generally listed: (1) a slump in business activity, (2) decline in gross production, especially in the automotive in-

---

[7] Gur'yev, *op cit.*, p. 36.

[8] I. D. Ivanov, "The Lessons of 1973-1975," in "The Economic Situation of the United States (A Scientific Conference)," *SShA*, No. 10 (October 1975), p. 60.

[9] Yu. I. Bobrakov, "The Long-Drawn-Out Character of the Withdrawal from the Crisis," in *ibid.*, p. 53.

dustry, (3) the highest unemployment in postwar years, (4) an unrestrained rise in prices, (5) the further devaluation of the dollar on the international currency market, (6) runaway inflation, (7) energy problems, (8) increased conflicts between labor and capital, and (9) the decline of real wages.[10] Considering all these factors, points out D. Kostyukhin, the deputy director of the Market Studies Institute of the USSR Ministry of Foreign Trade, "the present crisis eclipses all the previous postwar economic perturbations in the various capitalist countries or the capitalist world economy as a whole."[11]

A unique feature of the present crisis, note Soviet analysts, is its geographic breadth. Unlike other postwar crises, the present one extends simultaneously to practically all of the major capitalist countries. Thus, the factors leading to the asynchrony of the crisis cycles of capitalist countries are gradually losing their force, and the factors leading to a synchronization of crisis cycles are becoming considerably stronger.[12] The result is that capitalist crises are no longer isolated phenomena, but have become mutually reinforcing.

Numerous Soviet authors have taken note that the present crisis is not solely an economic crisis. It is claimed, rather, that capitalism is experiencing problems in a wide range of fields. As one such writer has remarked:

> It would be a mistake to regard the present difficulties only from the economic angle—as another cyclical crisis of overproduction that has hit all capitalist countries. For it is not only an economic

---

10 See, for example, the lead article in *Izvestiya*, January 30, 1975; V. M. Kudrov, department head at IMEMO, "Some Issues of the Economic Competition of the USSR and the USA," *SShA*, No. 9 (September 1975), p. 17; Y. Kvashnin and G. Nikolayev, "Class Battles under Détente," *International Affairs* (Moscow), No. 9 (September 1975), p. 110; V. Martynov, deputy director of IMEMO, "The World Nature of the Economic Crisis," in "Economic Crisis in the World of Capitalism (Discussion at the Academic Council of the Institute of World Economics and International Relations)," *Mirovaya Ekonomika i Mezhdunarodnyye Otnosheniya*, No. 4 (April 1975), p. 15; Yu. Pokatayev, "The USA: The Crisis Deepens," in *ibid.*, p. 23; and S. V. Safronov, department chief of the Scientific Research Institute of Business Cycles (NIKI) of the Ministry of Foreign Trade, "The Situation in the American Economy," *SShA*, No. 3 (March 1975), p. 3.

11 D. Kostyukhin, "The Great Depression of the Seventies," *New Times* (Moscow), No. 26 (June 1975), p. 18.

12 V. Martynov, deputy director of IMEMO, "A Concluding Word," in "Economic Crisis in the World of Capitalism (Discussion at the Academic Council of the Institute of World Economics and International Affairs)," *Mirovaya Ekonomika i Mezhdunarodnyye Otnosheniya*, No. 6 (June 1975), pp. 101-02.

recession but a crisis of their social, political and ideological struggle. It is an eruption of all the contradictions inherent in the development of modern state monopoly capitalism.[13]

In sum, it is of such a "profound nature" that it "embraces all aspects of life in the capitalist countries."[14]

According to traditional Marxist-Leninist theory, capitalism is incapable of preventing the occurrence of periodic crises, because such crises arise from the "basic contradiction" of the capitalist socioeconomic system, namely, "the contradiction between the social nature of production and the private capitalist form of appropriation of the results of production."[15] Despite this predilection to emphasize the debased condition of capitalism, however, Moscow's spokesmen exclude the implication that the collapse of the capitalist system is imminent. Indeed, as one Soviet writer points out, the present crisis "is cyclical and therefore transient."[16] Still, there is much ambiguity as to the time frame when the United States may be expected to begin its recovery from the present crisis. For example, during the second joint scientific conference of IUSAC and IMEMO, one analyst cautiously suggested that "the 'bottom' of the crisis, so it seems, has passed by,"[17] while another predicted that "an upsurge phase *[faza pod"yema]* will set in no earlier than 1977."[18]

The U.S. Role in the Internationalization of Capitalism

Russian analysts regard the United States as being responsible for the introduction and growth of a new factor in international capitalism which may bring about short-term economic gains but carries within it the seeds of capitalism's ultimate demise: the internationalization of the capitalist economic structure through multinational

---

13 Kostyukhin, *op cit.*, p. 18.

14 A. Grechikhin, "The Economy of Socialism and Capitalism in the First Half of the 1970s," *Mirovaya Ekonomika i Mezhdunarodnyye Otnosheniya*, No. 2 (February 1976), p. 6.

15 S. Menshikov, professor and doctor of economic sciences, *The Economic Cycle: Postwar Developments* (Moscow: Progress Publishers, 1975), p. 10. Cf. Yu. Pokatayev and V. Shenayev, "Some Features of the Contemporary Economic Crisis," *Kommunist*, No. 12 (August 1975), p. 85.

16 S. A. Dalin, "The Contemporary World Economic Crisis and the Economy of the USA," *SShA*, No. 8 (August 1975), p. 20.

17 Ivanov, *op. cit.*, p. 60.

18 Bobrakov, *op. cit.*, p. 54.

corporations, referred to by the Soviets as "international monopolies." Soviet specialists identify three basic groups of such "monopolies":

- Military-industrial monopolies, most of whose output consists of armaments contracted for by the government;

- Monopolies with large overseas investments or marketing a considerable part of their products overseas and thereby requiring political safeguards for their interests in foreign countries;

- Monopolies which, because of their insignificant overseas sales and investments, are mainly interested in economic stability in the United States itself and less concerned with the political problems affecting other countries.[19]

According to some Soviet analysts, the first category dominated the U.S. economy through the Vietnam War period of the 1960s and early 1970s, but "lately, there has been a marked growth in the influence exercised by the second group of monopolies."[20] Moreover, it is stated that the subordination of the status of the military-industrial monopolies to the multinational corporations "constitutes one of the chief factors in the charting of U.S. foreign policy strategy for the 1970s."[21]

The Soviets believe that contradictory processes are emerging from the nature of U.S. capitalism, which the multinational corporations only exacerbate. While reduction of the defense budget and concomitantly of defense contracts would be anti-inflationary, such a reduction, in the Soviet view, leads to unemployment and worsens the recession. Furthermore, the activity of the multinational corporations has contributed to deficits in the U.S. balance of payments, as well as to further unemployment of American workers and a growth of contradictions between the United States, on the one hand, and both the developing countries and America's allies, on the other. Soviet spokesmen conclude from this that "the domestic and international needs of state monopoly capitalism in the United States are interconnected" and the current situation truly demonstrates the

---

19 Anatoliy Gromyko and A. Kokoshin, "U.S. Foreign Policy Strategy for the 1970s," *International Affairs*, No. 10 (October 1973), p. 68.
20 *Ibid.*
21 *Ibid.*, p. 69. The third group of monopolies—those whose orientations are primarily domestic—is regarded as inconsequential and is not dealt with in any detail.

exploitative nature of U.S. capitalism; only the monopolies "have increased their profits," while the country itself is having difficulty "making ends meet."[22]

According to Soviet officials, U.S. corporations with interests abroad can no longer rely upon American military-political intervention in their behalf, due to the reduced capabilities of the United States in light of the decisive shift which has occurred in the correlation of world forces. Therefore, those U.S.-based multinational corporations which formerly represented the interests of the country as a whole have assumed a transnational character—that is, they have circumvented the traditional jurisdiction of the nation-state—and the American economy has correspondingly reaped diminshed returns from these companies' profits. Investment capital of the multinational corporations tends to find its way into opportune areas of Europe, Asia and the Third World, rather than stimulating U.S. domestic employment and production. This process has further exacerbated an already unstable monetary relationship among the capitalist states, in the Soviet view, since these corporations, having divorced their interests from those of the United States, often put themselves into competitive positions with the latter. Furthermore, their predominance provides the multinational corporations with leverage by which they can influence Washington, but without the high degree of symbiosis which at one time had characterized business-governmental relations.[23]

Capitalism and the Revolution in Science and Technology

Soviet spokesmen concede that the United States presently holds superiority in the areas of science and technology (S&T), "especially in their practical application."[24] Yet capitalism is seen to be inherently incapable of fully and effectively utilizing the fruits of the S&T revolution.

---

[22] Viktor Perlo, "The Latest Outbreak of a Chronic Disease," *Izvestiya*, September 14, 1974; Pokatayev, *op. cit.*

[23] See M. Maksimova, *Economic Aspects of Capitalist Integration* (Moscow: Progress Publishers, 1973), pp. 50-63; Gromyko and Kokoshin, *op. cit.*, pp. 67-73; Mileykovskiy, *op. cit.*

[24] Kudrov, *op. cit.*, p. 19.

> . . . the scientific-technological revolution is a powerful ally of socialism, [but] under capitalist conditions the collectivization of its production erodes further and further the foundations of the existing order, and gives birth to new forms of antagonisms.[25]

Soviet analyses of the present economic crisis take into account, therefore, that the great production capability generated by American S&T might dissipate many current economic problems. However, it is uniformly posited that such success will foster a temporary recovery only, and in the longer term, the S&T revolution will provoke new crises.

These new crises, it is maintained, will be more severe because science and technology are incapable of eradicating the conflicts and contradictions inherent in the capitalist system.[26] In fact, F. Konstantinov, a member of the USSR Academy of Sciences, has observed that "as has been revealed in recent decades, the scientific and technological revolution has sharpened the old contradictions of capitalist society and generated new ones."[27] Thus, it is argued that the impact of S&T is directly linked with the intensification and aggravation of the class struggle,[28] chiefly because S&T "undermines the foundations of the obsolete social system" of capitalism.[29] Particularly vivid is the description of the supposed effects of the S&T revolution on the individual in capitalist society. Writing in *Kommunist*, one Soviet doctor of philosophical sciences asserted:

> The scientific-technical revolution by its course reveals the most morbid and inherent feature of capitalist society: its hostility to man, the individual, to spiritual culture in general, its Shylock passion to utilize for the sake of profit not only a man's blood but also the living soul and his beating heart. Against the background of the unparalleled scale of the growth of material wealth and the tremendous technological and scientific achievements of capitalism,

---

25 B. N. Ponomarev, "Topical Problems in the Theory of the World Revolutionary Process," *Kommunist*, No. 15 (October 1971), p. 40.
26 M. Volkov, "Scientific and Technological Revolution and the Creation of the Material and Technical Basis of Communism," *Social Sciences* (Moscow), VII, No. 1 (1976), 38-39.
27 *Pravda*, September 12, 1974.
28 G. Nikolayev, "Scientific and Technological Progress and the Class Struggle," *International Affairs* (Moscow), No. 5 (May 1974), p. 87.
29 D. Tomashevskiy, "The Scientific and Technological Revolution and U.S. Foreign Policy," *Kommunist*, No. 2 (January 1975).

the depreciation of the value of human development becomes particularly striking. . . .

Capital is a "great" psychologist. It does business not only by sapping the worker but in his exhaustion offering in abundance the means of spiritual stupefaction: cheap literature, shocking movie and television hackwork, low-quality shows, pornography, narcotics and hallucinogenics; consequently, it not only limits, but destroys the individual.[30]

Thus, summarizes one writer, the S&T revolution "exacerbates the contradictions of capitalist society and increases the material and technical preconditions for socialism."[31]

Soviet analysts perceive several general effects stemming from the influence of the S&T revolution on capitalist systems:

- The uneven development of production forces (the S&T revolution does not eliminate the tremendous gap in the development of industrial output between developed capitalist countries and developing countries);

- The distorted development of production forces;

- The militarization of capitalist production;

- The existence of crises and stagnation in the development of the economy;

- The predatory utilization of natural resources by capitalist monopolies, the poisoning of the environment and the deterioration of human living conditions;

- The monopolistic distribution of the social product and the inability of the capitalist world to resolve, under the conditions of highly developed production facilities, basic social problems, and to eliminate poverty, hunger and social and material insecurity.[32]

The impact of the S&T revolution on the American economy is viewed no less drastically. While the development and application of

---

[30] G. Volkov, "Karl Marx and the Problem of Man under Conditions of the Scientific-Technological Revolution," *Kommunist,* No. 13 (September 1975), pp. 51-52.

[31] B. Bessonov, "The Scientific and Technological Revolution and the Ideological Struggle," *International Affairs* (Moscow), No. 2 (February 1974), p. 69.

[32] I. A. Kozikov, "Problems of the Correlation Between the Scientific and Technical and Social Revolutions," *Nauchnyy Kommunizm* (Scientific Communism), in JPRS, *Translations on USSR Political and Sociological Affairs,* No. 450 (October 31, 1973), pp. 40-41.

S&T speeds up the use of advanced technology in the production process, it at the same time introduces destabilizing forces which disrupt the economy:

> The scientific and technical revolution accelerates the practical utilization of new equipment and new technological ways and processes, the use of new materials and so on. In turn this creates drastic changes in correlations among economic sectors and spheres, and among the different elements of the production process; it destroys the established system of production organization, and triggers profound structural changes in the economy as a whole, and in industry in particular.[33]

In addition, the Russians have perceived a number of specific trends occurring as a result of S&T developments. Among these is the substantially changing distribution of manpower in basic sectors of the economy: a decrease in the number of people employed in the agricultural and extracting sectors and an increase in the number of people employed in processing and services. Also, the new industrial sectors, which exploit the trends of S&T progress, develop more rapidly than the others. These sectors include electrical engineering and electronics, sectors of aerospace and nuclear industries.

Détente and the U.S. Economic Crisis

Given the alleged crisis of American capitalism at the present time, Soviet spokesmen offer détente as the only palliative for the American economy. In contrast, Soviet analysts say that "the real facts" indicate that the Soviet Union does not have "economic motives" for seeking a relaxation of tension.

> It is not the socialist countries but the world of capitalism which is experiencing increasing economic and financial difficulties in the heart of its economy. All realistically minded politicians in the West, not to mention representatives of the business world, are talking about the desirability and necessity of developing trade and economic ties with the socialist states, not least because this is dictated by the vital interests of the Western countries themselves.[34]

---

[33] L. Leont'yev, "A Study of Capitalism in the 1970s," *Kommunist*, No. 10 (July 1974), pp. 120-21.
[34] V. Matveyev, "The Logic of Life—The Relaxation of Tension and Soviet-American Relations," *Izvestiya*, November 23, 1974.

In essence, détente is claimed to be "simply essential" for the United States; American opponents of the principles of peaceful coexistence who assert that the USSR will receive unilateral benefit from the relationship are said to hurt U.S. interests alone.

> The Soviet Union became a mighty industrial modern power without help from outside. Anyone who really believes that the future of the Soviet economy depends on American technology is thinking like a small shopkeeper. Judging by what we now read in the American press, it is the American and not the Soviet economy that is in dire straits.[35]

The solution for the United States, as suggested by the Soviets, comes in the form of a linkage between U.S. economic interests and the political prospects offered by Soviet-American détente. It is claimed that such an American dependency upon the Soviet Union will provide a shield for the United States, allowing America to adjust to the new realities in world politics and economy, characterized by "the Soviet Union's tremendous economic potential and the breadth of [its] economic relations with the European countries and Japan."[36]

The Crisis of Bourgeois Ideology

While in the Soviet interpretation the policy of peaceful coexistence entails some degree of cooperation between East and West in the political, economic, military (especially arms control) and scientific-technological spheres,[37] Soviet leaders adamantly assert that "in the field of ideology there is not and cannot be peaceful coexistence between socialism and capitalism."[38] Indeed, Soviet officials contend that the decisive shift in the correlation of forces has necessitated that capitalist-imperialist methods for attacking the socialist system

---

35 Valentin Zorin, commentary on Radio Moscow International Service, February 15, 1975.
36 N. Patolichev, Minister of Foreign Trade of the USSR, "An Important Factor of Peace and Progress: The Present Stage of the Soviet Union's Trade and Economic Relations with the Countries of the West," *Pravda*, April 9, 1975.
37 N. S. Khrushchev, speech in Moscow, *Pravda*, December 30, 1955; L. I. Brezhnev, speech in Moscow at World Conference of Communist and Workers' Parties, *Pravda*, June 8, 1969.
38 Editorial, "The Pressing Tasks of Ideological Work," *Pravda*, July 8, 1972.

must increasingly take ideological form, as opportunities for using "positions of strength" methods diminish. As Brezhnev stated shortly after the May 1972 Moscow summit meeting:

> Striving for the confirmation of the principle of peaceful coexistence, we recognize that successes in this important matter in no way signify the possibility of weakening the ideological struggle. On the contrary, it is necessary to be prepared that this struggle will intensify, will become a still sharper form of the antagonism between the two social systems. And we do not have any doubts about the outcome of this struggle, for the truth of history, the objective laws of social development are on our side.[39]

In the light of this viewpoint, it is not surprising that the greater frequency of Soviet contacts with foreigners, which has arisen as an unavoidable by-product of détente, has prompted strident warnings concerning the necessity for increased vigilance in the ideological sphere. Soviet citizens are cautioned about the subversive potential of visiting (especially U.S.) tourists, businessmen, scientists and journalists in the USSR and are made particularly aware that seemingly harmless "bridge-building" and "convergence" theories—which preach the forbidden idea of ideological coexistence—are designed "to befuddle the masses, to blunt their social consciousness."[40] In fact, G. A. Arbatov, in the first issue of IUSAC's journal, wrote the following:

> Even such forms of international intercourse as trade, cultural and scientific-technical ties and so on, which are generally accepted and have enjoyed a good reputation for centuries, when passed through the thinking meat grinder of these people [i.e., capitalists] are immediately turned into their antipode, into sinister weapons of subversive activity.[41]

With regard to ideological competition, in the Soviet view, bourgeois ideology—like its "class" progenitor, bourgeois economy—will eventually lose its force, due to the immutability of the processes which govern social development globally. In the words of Brezh-

---

[39] *Pravda*, June 28, 1972. See also B. N. Ponomarev, speech at All-Army Conference of Ideological Workers, *Krasnaya Zvezda*, January 29, 1975.

[40] Brezhnev, speech at World Conference of Communist and Workers' Parties, *op. cit.*

[41] G. A. Arbatov, "American Foreign Policy at the Threshold of the 1970s," *SShA*, No. 1 (January 1970), p. 25. See also V. Kudinov and V. Pletnikov, "Relaxation of Tension and Maneuvers of Anti-Communism," *Pravda*, August 9, 1974.

nev, "Marxism-Leninism is on the offensive today, and we must develop that offensive to the utmost."[42] However, Soviet leaders believe that capitalist-imperialists, aware of the bankruptcy and futility of their ideology, will try to compensate for these inherent weaknesses of bourgeois ideology by "using the most refined methods of ideological subversion."[43] Thus, Soviet spokesmen claim that recognition of the "objective realities" by U.S. leaders and their abandonment of such Cold War strategies as "rollback," "massive retaliation" and "brinkmanship" in the political-military sphere, as well as of blatant anti-communism, have led to this refinement of subversion in the period of Soviet-American détente:

> ... in view of the manifest failure of the previous strategy and the ineffectiveness of military strong-arm methods in relations with the socialist countries—the "bridge-building" concept, which regarded the establishment of peaceful relations with the countries of the world socialist system chiefly as a means for weakening and disuniting it, became quite widespread in the West.[44]

Western "bridge building" is really but a bourgeois tactic of "silent counterrevolution," a major purpose being "to wrest [the Eastern European] countries from the socialist community, to restore capitalism in them and to undermine the might of world socialism," as in the case of Czechoslovakia.[45] Advocates of convergence theories (including those who foresee the "end of ideology," "post-industrial society," "industrial society" or "technotronic society"), according to Soviet analysts, preach a form of "positive" anti-communism, in that they attempt to subvert socialist society with anti-Marxist concepts of the future world order.

Equally dangerous to the Soviets are the "negative," or overt, anti-Communists, who are said to oppose détente per se or to try, at the very least, to use it for exerting leverage upon the Soviet Union

---

42 Brezhnev, speech at World Conference of Communist and Workers' Parties, *op. cit.*
43 M. A. Suslov, speech to the Sixth Congress of the All-Union "Znaniye" Society, *Pravda*, June 21, 1972.
44 D. Tomashevskiy, "Toward a Radical Restructuring of International Relations," *MEIMO*, No. 1 (January 1975), pp. 4-5.
45 Academicians A. Rumyantsev and M. Mitin and Doctor of Philosophical Sciences M. Mshveniyeradze, "The Urgent Questions of the Struggle Against Anti-Communism," *Pravda*, October 13, 1969; also V. Rumyantsev, "Complex Events and Simple Truths," *Izvestiya*, October 3, 1968; Lieutenant General A. Shevchenko, "An Insidious Weapon," *Krasnaya Zvezda*, August 18, 1972.

in order to transform the Soviet internal structure. An analysis written at the end of 1974 describes this group as a "strange coalition"

> . . . whose members markedly activated their attempts to "abolish détente" on the eve of and after the change in U.S. Presidents, which occurred in extraordinary circumstances. . . . Under the pretext of "establishing limits to détente" they strove to liquidate the fundamental turnabout which has taken place in Soviet-U.S. relations . . . under the fabricated pretext that the agreements reached in this sphere allegedly give "one-sided advantages" to the Soviet Union.[46]

The coalition of anti-Communist Americans who are advocating policies "contrary to the spirit of the times" includes "the military-industrial complex, ultra-right and Zionist circles, the reactionary leadership of the AFL-CIO trade union association and certain journalistic circles." Their aim, like that of the convergence theorists, is to cause "erosion" of the Communist system, although by means of more direct tactics, such as the Jackson Amendment.[47]

Despite the "slanders" of bourgeois ideology directed against socialist society, Moscow claims that the ideological competition between the two systems has caused more harm to capitalist society than to the Soviet Union, partly because of the successful Soviet campaign for vigilance against capitalist ideological subversion. The Soviets assert that their task of guarding against capitalist ideology will be made easier in the future since there is a "growing feeling of protest against spiritual impoverishment which is spreading to wider and wider sectors" of the intelligentsia in the capitalist countries, "a factor which is undermining the ideological foundations of the capitalist world."[48] In general, Soviet leaders perceive the contradictions of bourgeois ideology and the associated "moral crisis" in the West as having far-reaching and almost catastrophic consequences for the

---

[46] Editorial, "The Vladivostok Meeting," *SShA*, No. 12 (December 1974), pp. 4-5.

[47] Colonel K. Payusov, "Behind the Facade of the 'Open Society,'" *Krasnaya Zvezda*, July 25, 1974; L. I. Brezhnev, speech at World Peace Congress in Moscow, *Pravda*, October 27, 1973. (The Jackson Amendment denied most-favored-nation status to the USSR because of restrictions on the emigration of Soviet citizens.)

[48] Ye. D. Modrzhinskaya and Ts. A. Stepanyan, *The Future of Society: A Critique of Modern Bourgeois Philosophical and Sociopolitical Conceptions* (Moscow: Progress Publishers, 1973), p. 308. Also editorial article, "Leninism—The Ideological Weapon of the Working People," *Vestnik Akademii Nauk SSSR* (Herald of the Academy of Sciences of the USSR), No. 3 (March 1970), pp. 3-13.

capitalist countries. Brezhnev, at a ceremony in the Moldavian SSR in late 1974, stated that "perhaps at no time during the past ten years has the crisis of bourgeois democracy, accelerating the disintegration of the political machinery of capitalist rule, been so obvious." Moreover, he pointed out that a characteristic feature of bourgeois ideology—"indifference to the fate of mankind"—is repelling the masses, particularly the youth, in the West.[49]

Some American leaders, said to be sensing the impending collapse of the moral bases of their society, react angrily and lash out at the Soviet Union, Such anti-communism is, therefore, a "weapon of the doomed."[50] Other American leaders, the "sober realists" in the U.S. political and business leadership, are said to have adapted to the "new global conditions" of waning U.S. power vis-à-vis the Soviet Union by accepting the principles of peaceful coexistence. However, the form of bourgeois ideological defense is inconsequential. All are doomed to defeat by the law-governed processes of social change.

Sociopolitical Forces in the American Class Struggle

Class struggle, led by the proletariat and directed toward a transformation from bourgeois to socialist rule is regarded by Marxist-Leninists as an inevitable process. The type of struggle, whether peaceful or violent, is said to be dependent on the nature and strength of bourgeois opposition. Even détente, noted Brezhnev at the 25th CPSU Congress, "does not in the slightest way abolish nor can it abolish or alter the laws of class struggle."[51] Indeed, Brezhnev alleged that, because of the "proletarian" activity of the working class in capitalist states, the class struggle was being heightened and the threat to the basic norms and institutions of bourgeois society was intensifying. In conjunction with this perception, Soviet analysts of the American sociopolitical scene strive to provide evidence of the existence of "revolutionary forces" in the United States and to illustrate that these forces have a significant impact on the class struggle.

---

49 *Pravda*, October 12, 1974.
50 G. A. Arbatov, *The War of Ideas in Contemporary International Relations* (Moscow: Progress Publishers, 1973), p. 129.
51 *Pravda*, February 25, 1976.

As an ideology oriented toward the working class, Marxism-Leninism places heavy emphasis on an evaluation of those forces which tend to undermine the ability of the so-called "bourgeois monopolist" clique to maintain its control over American society. Among these forces are listed such diverse groups and elements as: American labor, the youth movement, ethnic minorities, the women's liberation movement, liberals and public opinion. In addition, much polemical criticism is directed toward those groups and elements which support the ruling elite: the military-industrial complex, reactionaries, Zionists and anti-Communists. The more important of these groups and forces are discussed in the following sections.

THE LABOR MOVEMENT

Soviet assessments claim that the workers' movement is gathering momentum because the American political and socioeconomic system increasingly has failed to satisfy the needs of the workers.[52] Thus, it is claimed that the clashes between the workers and the representatives of the state-monopolistic sector "are assuming an ever more adamant character and wide scope" and that "the wave of protest" against monopolist policies is growing. To prove this point one Soviet writer alludes to the increasing number of people involved in and the lengthening average duration of the strike movement in the United States and he then concludes:

> A trend was thus confirmed which has become characteristic since the beginning of the 1970s: the cyclical factor of economic development no longer has as much influence on the dynamics of the labor movement as previously. Even high unemployment does not reduce strike activity. This indicates a radicalization of the workers' movement in the face of the increasing erosion of the toilers' income as a result of inflation.[53]

---

[52] For examples of Soviet thinking on this subject, see A. A. Popov, *Gosudarstvo i profsoyuzy* (The State and the Trade Unions) (Moscow: "Nauka," 1974), pp. 210-18; N. V. Mostovets, "Certain Aspects of the U.S. Labor Movement," *SShA*, No. 3 (March 1971), pp. 10-26; and E. Kuzmin, " 'Eternal Problems' of the American Society," *International Affairs*, No. 5 (May 1975), pp. 61-68.

[53] A. Iskenderov, "On the Class Battles in the Citadels of Capitalism," *Kommunist*, No. 9 (June 1974), p. 111.

Still, it is asserted that the labor movement is hindered by the fact that the trade unions, the largest mass organizations of the workers, are dominated by individuals who betray the proletariat by supporting the capitalist economic system, as well as imperialist and anti-Soviet policies. Moreover, in saying that "the leadership of many unions defends capitalism and carries out bourgeois policies in the ranks of the working class," specific reference is given to the anti-Soviet policies advocated by George Meany:

> In the American trade union movement, there is a group of trade unions where these conservative trends and the traditions of so-called "commercial unionism" are especially strong. This group makes up the strong "conservative nucleus" in the AFL-CIO and a kind of base for the leading bosses of the AFL-CIO. It is precisely on the conservative trade unions that Meany primarily leans in implementing his domestic and foreign policy course.[54]

Thus despite the alleged intensification of the class struggle, and the role of the proletariat in the van of the "progressive" forces, Soviet analysts appear to recognize that conservative labor organizations and their "reactionary" leaders will maintain their influence over the ranks of American labor. Therefore the character of the American labor movement will remain "reformist," which, while representative of a progressive trend, falls far short of and indeed undermines the dynamic conditions necessary for the transformation to socialism.

THE YOUTH MOVEMENT

Among the mass movements compelling the scrutiny and provoking the interest of Soviet Americanologists is the American youth movement. Seen to compose, during the 1960s, along with students and progressive intelligentsia, the nucleus of America's "democratic forces,"[55] the youth movement

---

54 V. A. Aleksandrova, "The Strike Struggle in 1975," *SShA*, No. 2 (June 1974), pp. 96-97.

55 I. G. Samoshova, review article, in *SShA*, No. 2 (February 1975), p. 98, on *Ob-shchestvenno-politicheskiye dvizheniya v SShA, 60-ye-nacholo 70-kh godov* (Social-Political Movements in the United States of America—1960s to the Beginning of the 1970s), edited by M. S. Vozchikov, S. M. Zagladina, N. V. Mostovets and S. A. Drabkina (Moscow: Politizdat, 1974).

... acquired a clearly manifested political nature of opposition to the dominance of the monopolies and militarism. This movement has a great potential for involving the broad masses in the struggle for revolutionary changes.[56]

The rise of the youth movement and the tensions it created in U.S. society are viewed by Soviet analysts as a consequence of the intensifying ideological-political crisis threatening the basic ideals, norms and institutions of bourgeois society:

> The problem of American youth is the problem of the total failure of the ideals of American society and the disillusionment of its most sensitive segment with such ideals, for the propagation of which to the whole world, the American bourgeoisie has used up so much of its means and force. Even though the opposition to these false ideals carries at the present time a character often spontaneous, inconsistent, sometimes naïve, most often totally unorganized, the mass character of this protest, its activism, testifies to the fact that we speak here of the ideological, spiritual, and political crisis of the American bourgeoisie, which pretended to the role of universal leader and which turned out to be unable to lead even the young generation of its own country.[57]

The more radical elements of the youth movement, including students and intelligentsia, as well as radical factions among racial minorities, were classified by Soviet analysts under the general rubric of "New Left." The phenomenon of the "New Left" was assessed as comprising more than a "manifestation of petty-bourgeois student radicalism," and was viewed as "a special ideological and political position of protesting students and intellectuals, reflecting the process whereby working intellectuals are converted into a force

---

[56] L. Yakovlev and A. Antonov, "O Rabochem i demokraticheskom dvizhenii v SShA," Kommunist, No. 11 (July 1973), p. 127, a review of SShA: Sotsial'no-politicheskiy krizis, problemy rabochego i demokraticheskogo dvizheniya (USA: Sociopolitical Crisis and Problems of the Workers' and Democratic Movements) (Moscow: "Nauka," 1972).

[57] SShA: Problemy vnutrenney politiki (USA: Domestic Political Problems) (Moscow: "Nauka," 1971), pp. 20-21. This work was prepared by the USSR Academy of Sciences author collective, under the direction of V. S. Zorin, Doctor of Historical Sciences.

opposed to capitalism."[58] Soviet discussions of the youth movement and "New Left" in particular are generally critical in tone, stressing the internal disorder, anarchistic tendencies, ideological vagueness, organizational confusion and nihilism which sapped the effectiveness of these groups. For all their inherent weaknesses, such movements were noted as positive manifestations of the socioeconomic, political and ideological changes convulsing American society, stemming from the scientific-technological revolution under the conditions of state monopoly capitalism and from the influence of world socialism and the national liberation movement.[59]

Specific criticisms of the "New Left" include the charge that it "denied the necessity of defining a clear ideological position," and therefore "many different political forces were often acting in their midst."[60] Additional problems and contradictions of the "New Left" are enumerated in a monograph prepared by the staff members of the USSR Academy of Sciences Institute for the Study of the United States and Canada (IUSAC), which observed among other things:

> The "New Left" had a negative outlook toward organization, and rejected political struggle. They didn't have a clear positive program, and their views about the way to reorganize the world were very confused and eclectic. The initial ideological-political basis of the "New Left" presented a contradictory picture, where left extremism and calls for immediate revolution appeared together with reformism, while nihilism, anarchism, the denial of organization and political struggle were combined with a utopian program for the building of an idyllic society of "democratic participation," and elements of liberalism with its idiosyncratic organizational variety.[61]

Moscow acknowledges that the youth movement was closely connected with the general antiwar movement of the Vietnam period,

---

58 N. S. Ivanov, review article, in *SShA*, No. 6 (June 1975), p. 100, on *SShA: Studenty i politika amerikanskoye studenchestvo v demokraticheskoy bor'be v 60-70c Gody* (USA: Students and Politics—The American Students in the Democratic Struggle of the 1960s and 1970s), edited by V. S. Zorin and L. A. Salcheva (Moscow: "Nauka," 1974).

59 *Ibid.*, p. 99.

60 Zorin and Salycheva, *op. cit.*, p. 51.

61 *Ibid.*

and that since the end of the war there has been a general decline in protest and political activities on the part of the young. This decline is attributed to government efforts at both reform and repression, to the end of American involvement in the war and to the inherent contradictions of the youth movement itself. With respect to the student movement, however, a group of Soviet authors observed:

> The end of the rise of the student movement in the United States did not mean the diminishing of its force. Despite the decline of strong student organizations into extreme fragmentation, the students of the 1970s preserve their activist character.[62]

PUBLIC OPINION

In examining the complex and competing influences on American public opinion, Soviet analysts pay close attention to public opinion polls.[63] While Soviet observers contend that public opinion does not directly influence the formulation of U.S. foreign policy, they assert that American politicians follow the polls with great interest.

> Government officials in the United States are interested in analysis of the results of public opinion surveys not so much because they want to take into account the attitude of the public in formulation of the course of government policy as because they want to try to obtain information about how they should conduct their propaganda work in order to alter tendencies in public opinion that are unfavorable to the country's ruling circles: what aspect and what strata of the public they should aim at, and how intensively they need to wage this propaganda.[64]

In spite of such qualifications, and with frequent warnings that public opinion polls help the bourgeoisie retain control over the exploited American masses, Soviet sources occasionally quote the results of such polls with great satisfaction. In the summer of 1973, for example, one Soviet observer cited American polls concerning attitudes toward the Soviet Union, noting that the number of American

---

[62] *Ibid.*, p. 97.
[63] For a historical treatment of the development of opinion polling in the United States, see M. M. Petrovskaya, "Public Opinion Polls in the United States," *Voprosy Istorii* (Problems of History), No. 2 (February 1976), pp. 113-23.
[64] E. A. Ivanyan, "Public Opinion: Its Role in Political Life," *SShA*, No. 8 (August 1974), pp. 25-26.

citizens who were favorably disposed toward the USSR in 1973 was twenty-one times that of 1954 and ten times as large as in 1967.[65]

Employing the results of public opinion polls, analyses of congressional spending and discussions of antiwar demonstrations, Soviet sources contend that "even U.S. militarists have had to call public opinion their Achilles' heel."[66] This crisis in public opinion is attributed directly to the Vietnam War. The "liberal bourgeoisie," the "realistic circles" and the "honest intellectuals," according to Moscow, were so outraged by the war that they lost their confidence in the wisdom of Washington's foreign policy.[67] Further proof of this favorable trend, in Soviet eyes, was provided by the "Cold War revisionists," who in varying degrees blamed the United States for causing Soviet-American tensions. As one Soviet source commented, never before in history had the American masses so doubted Washington's foreign policy as they did over the war in Vietnam.[68]

THE MILITARY-INDUSTRIAL COMPLEX

Soviet observers contend that the military-industrial complex also enjoys vast power over American public opinion, since it influences the communications media and can thus manipulate the sources of information available to the American people, and because millions of American jobs now depend directly on perpetuating the arms race. Thus, according to the Soviets, many working-class Americans, not to mention the lower ranks of the bourgeoisie, fearing the loss of their jobs, are compelled to support America's reactionary policies abroad.[69]

The influence of the military-industrial complex is said to be all-pervasive in the realm of foreign policy, though it is difficult to pre-

---

[65] Editorial, "A Great New Step Forward," *SShA*, No. 8 (August 1973), p. 5.

[66] G. A. Trofimenko, "Militarism and the Domestic Policy Struggle," *SShA*, No. 1 (January 1972), p. 70.

[67] V. S. Guseva, "Books on Pentagon Crimes in Indochina," *SShA*, No. 2 (February 1972), pp. 85-87, refers to "several dozen" examples of such views and lists over twenty book titles.

[68] Yu. A. Shvedkov, review article, in *SShA*, No. 9 (September 1970), p. 82, on Robert E. Osgood *et al., America and the World,* and Paul Seabury and Aaron Wildavsky, *U.S. Foreign Policy.*

[69] G. N. Tsagalov, "The Military-Industrial Complex: Some General Aspects," *SShA*, No. 11 (November 1970), pp. 21-30.

cisely define and delineate the frequently indirect but extremely effective ways this influence is brought to bear.[70] Nevertheless, Russian analysts assert:

> The one thing that can be said is that with any foreign policy decisions, no matter how complex, tangled and secret the mechanism by which they are made may be, whether indirectly or invisibly, the military-industrial complex is present, sometimes exercising a decisive influence, sometimes making concessions, and sometimes, for many reasons, suffering failures and defeats, and waiting for more advantageous situations on reserve lines.[71]

Soviet analysts, drawing on the notable American writings on this subject, broadly define the concept "military-industrial complex":

> The military-industrial complex is not only a bloc of military-industrial forms and the armed forces. The military-industrial complex is a concept which is far more capacious. It also includes large groups of scientists working on Pentagon assignments, journalists defending the viewpoint of the military on any questions of policy, trade union bosses who do not disdain CIA gifts—in a word, all those who are . . . interested for reasons of "skimming off the cream of patriotism" in preserving the "cold war" situation. This concept also includes such phenomena as the close personal union between the military elite, the government bureaucracy and the industrial leaders.[72]

According to Soviet formulations, the military-industrial complex constitutes only a portion of the bourgeois class which rules America. Nevertheless, it is a group which is most dangerous for world peace, for the USSR and for the American people themselves. Soviet scholars argue that the military-industrial complex has twin goals: to regain American military supremacy and to enrich itself by developing weapons for the U.S. government and selling arms abroad. It is claimed that since the most effective way to attain these ends is through a never-ending arms race, the military-industrial complex works unceasingly to control the American foreign policy appa-

---

[70] V. M. Mil'shteyn, *Voyenno-promyshlennyy kompleks i vneshnaya politika SShA* (The Military-Industrial Complex and United States Foreign Policy) (Moscow: "Mezhdunarodnyye Otnosheniya," 1975), p. 8.
[71] *Ibid.*
[72] Trofimenko, *op. cit.*, p. 66.

ratus. It employs several related techniques: subordinating the state machinery to the financial-industrial monopolies; supporting the most bellicose members of the U.S. government, whether in Congress or in the Executive Branch; and propagandizing about a supposed military threat from the Soviet Union.[73] Pressure from the military-industrial complex for higher profits and its intensified political influence give it an "enormous—and at certain stages, decisive" voice in U.S. foreign policy decisionmaking.

While the military-industrial complex is seen to remain a powerful influence on U.S. foreign policy, it must increasingly contend with the more moderate and sober elements of the ruling class. Since the reelection of President Nixon in 1972, Soviet sources have pointed to the debate in America over foreign policy as proof of the extreme polarization of the American bourgeoisie: while President Nixon and others of the ruling faction favored détente, the military-industrial complex continued to exercise influence. Supported by Zionists and anti-Communists, it still had the power to sabotage trade agreements with the USSR, to interfere in Soviet domestic affairs by manipulating the issue of Jewish emigration and to win congressional approval for increasing military spending and the funding of new weapons systems. Such displays of strength, however, could not obscure the fact that

> It has become more difficult for the military-industrial complex to impose their ideas on society in which the main element, if not the only element, "of national security" is the repulsion of armed "threat" from outside. Many Americans have become convinced that in the atomic age military strength is not capable of serving as an effective means of achieving political goals in the international arena and that the arms race interferes with the solution not only of internal problems of America but also the majority of international problems with which mankind is faced in our time.[74]

Thus, according to Russian commentators, the tide of opinion in

---

[73] A. I. Daikin, review article, in *SShA*, No. 7 (July 1975), pp. 88-99, on G. M. Kuzmin, *Voyenno-promyshlennyye kontserny* (Military-Industrial Concerns) (Moscow: "Nauka," 1974). See also Yu. Isayeva, *Labirinty voyennogo biznesa* (The Labyrinths of Military Business) (Moscow: "Mezhdunarodnyye Otnosheniya," 1969).

[74] N. A. Dolgopolova, "Military Spending and Public Opinion," *SShA*, No. 2 (February 1975), p. 115.

the United States seems to be turning against the "reactionaries." Even the military-industrial complex itself is described as having split over the issue of détente. These are regarded as "progressive developments" which are said to reflect broad-based new attitudes toward foreign policy. Soviet analysts express hope that these political trends, while not yet irreversible, will convince Americans to support détente with increasing vigor.

ANTI-COMMUNISM AND ZIONISM

Anti-communism appears in a variety of ideological guises, according to Soviet spokesmen, but all have the same goal of defaming Marxism-Leninism. Right-wing anti-Communists, left-wing anti-Soviets and even the "end-of-ideology theorists" are seen by Soviet observers as sharing the same bourgeois objectives. Within the United States, these "reactionary" ideologists support the arms race and foster anti-Soviet propaganda, while internationally they seek to weaken the unity of the world Communist movement.[75]

Soviet sources assert that the Zionists play an especially dangerous role in influencing Washington's foreign policy. It is claimed that Zionism has its real center in the United States, where influential Jewish capitalists dominate the movement, buy Israeli bonds and invest profitably in Israel. They also hold anti-Soviet views and favor imperialist policies. Soviet sources claim that since the Arab-Israeli War of 1967, the Zionists have undertaken a special campaign to slander the USSR, allying themselves with Russian émigré groups, Ukrainian nationalists, fascists, other anti-Communists, racists and even anti-Semites.[76]

Within the United States, the Zionists are said to direct a wide range of propaganda, blackmail, threats and disinformation at American society. Although some "left-wing" Jews supposedly reject

---

75 V. Mshveniyeradze, *Anti-Communism Today* (Moscow: Progress Publishers, 1974); L. N. Moskvichov, *The End of Ideology Theory: Illusions and Reality: Critical Notes on a Fashionable Bourgeois Conception* (Moscow: Progress Publishers, 1974).

76 Hyman Lumer (editor of *Political Affairs*, the theoretical journal of the Communist Party, USA), "Zionism and Anti-Semitism in the United States," *SShA*, No. 9 (September 1970), pp. 25-35, and "Zionism and Monopoly Capital," *SShA*, No. 9 (September 1972), pp. 25-33. For more detailed analysis, see V. Bolshakov, *Anti-Communism, the Main Line of Zionism* (Moscow: Progress Publishers, 1972), and I. Ivanov, *Caution: Zionism!* (Moscow: Progress Publishers, 1971).

Zionism, Soviet sources contend that the "Jewish lobby" works with both the military-industrial complex and "reactionaries" of all sorts to arouse anti-Soviet sentiments.[77] The Jewish Defense League is condemned as a purely fascist and racist organization, whose members can count on sympathizers in the American government to punish them lightly, if at all, for their crimes of violence against Soviet diplomats in the United States.[78] When all these different sorts of influence are combined, the Zionists become "particularly valuable to the U.S. circles opposing the normalization of Soviet-American relations and international détente in general."[79]

The Conduct of American Foreign Policy

According to Soviet spokesmen, a new era in superpower relations began with the signing of the SALT accords and related agreements in Moscow in May 1972. America's decision to turn away from the old "discredited" Cold War policy of confrontation in favor of peaceful coexistence is viewed as one of the most significant developments in contemporary international politics. It is not surprising, therefore, that a dominant theme in Russian analyses of Soviet-American relations is peaceful coexistence or détente—its meaning, significance and future directions. Much attention has been directed toward explaining why the United States embarked on its new course. This has led to evaluations of the role of the President, the Congress and such organizations within the Executive Branch as the Department of Defense, the CIA and the State Department in the formulation and conduct of American national security policy. Of course, these Soviet analyses note with approval American supporters of détente and castigate its critics.

THE PRESIDENT AND THE CONGRESS

Soviet sources describe the President as the primary source of

---

[77] I. I. Mints *et al., Sionism: Teoriya i praktika* (Zionism: Theory and Practice) (Moscow: Politizdat, 1973).

[78] Hyman Lumer, " 'The Jewish Defense League'—Instrument of Reaction," *SShA*, No. 9 (September 1973), pp. 25-32.

[79] V. Meshcheryakov, "At the Service of U.S. Reaction," *International Affairs*, No. 2 (February 1975), p. 90.

both innovation and direction in U.S. foreign policy. They regard his party affiliation as unimportant, since the real line of demarcation in American politics is said to run within the parties, and not between them.[80] The President is presumed to respond quite consciously to the needs of the monopoly capitalists and financial oligarchs who paid for his election campaign, and his general policies are seen as governed by the socioeconomic "laws" of the national and international class struggle. American elections can still be crucial in determining the directions of foreign policy, however, since the various candidates for presidential or congressional office must compete for support from the ruling bourgeoisie, who are not united on all aspects of national security policy even though they share a hatred of communism. The result of this capitalist factional rivalry is a series of zigzags in U.S. foreign policy, especially during election campaigns and whenever the Pentagon's budget is presented to the Congress. The President, the Soviets write, tends to oscillate between the various views on national strategy, foreign policy and budget allocations for military purposes put forward by these ruling cliques.

Until the winter of 1971-72, Soviet analysts regarded Richard M. Nixon as a strong, effective, but profoundly anti-Communist President. He had allegedly tried a "turn to the right" in the elections of 1970, deliberately raising tensions with the Soviet Union, but he then concluded that public opinion increasingly opposed anti-Sovietism. More fundamentally, Soviet spokesmen state, in late 1971 President Nixon and Dr. Kissinger, sensing a profound change in the "correlation of world forces," sought a relaxation of Soviet-American relations. This relaxation first took the form of seeking to end U.S. trade restrictions directed against the USSR.[81] While congressional approval was not forthcoming on the trade issue, nevertheless Nixon's willingness to attend the May 1972 Moscow

---

[80] I. R. Bagrov, "On the Book by Theodore White," *SShA*, No. 7 (July 1970), p. 101. For two basic Soviet analyses of presidential power and of U.S. foreign policy formulation and implementation, see Yu. Shvedkov, ed., *SShA: Vneshnepoliti-cheskiy mekhanizm* (USA: The Foreign Policy Mechanism) (Moscow: "Nauka," 1972), and Iv. Sevost'yan, *Planirovaniye vneshney politiki v SShA* (The Planning of Foreign Policy in the USA) (Moscow: "Mezhdunarodnyye Otnosheniya," 1972).

[81] Ye. S. Shershnev, "Soviet-U.S. Trade: Problems and Possibilities," *SShA*, No. 4 (April 1972), pp. 3-14. See also Yu. P. Davydov, V. V. Zhurkin and V. S. Rudnev, eds., *Doctrina Niksona* (The Nixon Doctrine) (Moscow: "Nauka," 1972), pp. 28-29.

meetings and his role in the SALT agreements are acknowledged in Soviet sources. Nixon's foreign policy innovations are not attributed to his goodwill, however, but to his realism, both in the foreign and domestic areas. Both his recognition that the decisive shift in the "correlation of world forces" precluded U.S. victory in Vietnam or any other application of a "positions of strength" policy[82] and his need for a striking policy success in order to win the 1972 election[83] are claimed to be the primary factors motivating the Nixon détente policies. The U.S. Congress now became the major obstacle to détente, in the Soviet view, after the President had accepted the changed international situation and adjusted to it.

Prior to 1973, Soviet analysts consistently denigrated the importance of the U.S. Congress in the formulation and conduct of foreign policy. Congressional powers were described as minor, limited principally to imposing specific cuts in military spending and to influencing public opinion.[84] Some congressmen received high praise for opposing the Vietnam War, attacking the power of the military-industrial complex and favoring a reduction in Soviet-American tensions, yet Soviet sources doubted that the Congress could significantly limit presidential power.[85] At the most, they suggested that President Nixon was concerned about the power of the Democrats in Congress and had temporarily lost control over Republican congressmen. Soviet observers categorically denied that the rivalry between the President and the Congress could go very far, however, because "the President and the Congress are indeed not competitors but, rather, partners working in one and the same political direction."[86]

These views changed significantly after the fall of 1973. Soviet analysts were pleased to report that Congress overrode Nixon's veto

---

[82] G. A. Arbatov, "An Event of World Significance," *SShA*, No. 8 (August 1972), pp. 3-12.

[83] Soviet analysts expressed great sympathy for McGovern's antimilitary and anti-Vietnam War sentiments, but they also accused him more harshly than Nixon of "unscrupulous maneuvering" and claimed that his many mistakes had led them to expect his defeat. V. Zorin, "First Results of the Elections," *SShA*, No. 12 (December 1972), pp. 55-59.

[84] Ye. G. Kruglov, "The Military-Industrial Complex or 'State Management,'" *SShA*, No. 12 (December 1970), pp. 60-62.

[85] V. V. Kopytin, "Battle Around the Cooper-Church Amendment," *SShA*, No. 9 (September 1970), pp. 79-81.

[86] V. M. Solomatina, "Limits of the Foreign Policy Powers of Congress," *SShA*, No. 3 (March 1972), p. 91.

of the War Powers Act. This legislation was described as bringing about a major change in the balance of power within the U.S. political system.

> The law limiting the President's right to conduct a war without the concurrence of Congress has therefore proved to be both an epilogue and a prologue to many other important events. Despite its compromise wording, it is almost the equivalent of a constitutional amendment in importance.[87]

The Jackson Amendment of December 1973 confirmed Russian interpretations of the growth in congressional power, but its actual content outraged the Soviet government. By denying most-favored-nation status to the USSR (unless and until Moscow altered its restrictions on emigration), Congress had taken a very "reactionary" step. Soviet observers explained the Jackson Amendment as a ploy by the military-industrial complex to frustrate détente and thereby contradict the wishes of the American people.[88] Senator Jackson was seen as having a sinister ability to rally anti-Soviet forces and to coerce the American government.[89]

THE EXECUTIVE PROCESS IN FOREIGN POLICY

Soviet sources describe the National Security Council as the dominant institution in formulating U.S. foreign policy, and they examine presidential reorganizations of the NSC with great care. They are especially interested in the relative power of the departments and agencies which are represented on the NSC. In 1970 Anatoliy A. Gromyko described the Department of Defense and the CIA as the strongest members of the Executive Branch, with the State Department playing a distinctly minor role as coordinator and executor of foreign policy.[90] Especially since 1969, according to Soviet analysts, the State Department role in determining long-range policy had de-

---

[87] D. N. Konovalov and V. A. Savel'yev, "Action to Limit Presidential War Powers," *SShA*, No. 2 (February 1974), p. 97.

[88] V. V. Zhurkin, "Foreign Policy Debates: From 'Globalism' to 'Selectiveness,' " *SShA*, No. 6 (June 1974), pp. 19-29, and N. D. Turkatenko, "U.S. Corporations in the Context of Détente," *SShA*, No. 6 (June 1974), pp. 30-43.

[89] V. S. Anichkina, "Struggle in Congress on Soviet-American Relations," *SShA*, No. 6 (June 1974), pp. 78-81.

[90] A. A. Gromyko, "The Dilemmas of American Diplomacy," *SShA*, No. 6 (June 1970), pp. 14-22.

creased.[91] Nixon's contribution to the administrative control of U.S. foreign policy consisted of increasing the size of the NSC and making it respond more effectively to presidential control. Soviet observers asserted that Nixon had decreased the power of the State Department within the NSC in two ways: by raising the power of the military and by increasing the influence of the President's Adviser on National Security Affairs, Dr. Henry Kissinger.[92]

These views changed gradually but significantly, as Kissinger grew in strength and became personally identified with the policy of détente. Indeed, while opposition to détente by the military-industrial complex and by the Zionists was described as the primary reason for Nixon's reorganization of the NSC, Kissinger's appointment as Secretary of State led Soviet analysts to conclude that the State Department had risen in importance, and that Kissinger was keeping his position as National Security Adviser for use against anti-détente forces in the Department of Defense.[93]

Soviet sources have taken careful note of CIA-Department of Defense disagreements aired in congressional testimony. While Soviet observers usually miss no chance to castigate the CIA, describing it as the chief instrument of imperialism's secret war against the progressive forces in the world and as a special state within the American state,[94] when CIA and Department of Defense representatives contradicted each other during congressional debates on strategy in the Indian Ocean, Moscow reacted quite differently:

> . . . it may not be out of place to recall the recent testimony by CIA director W. Colby to the Senate Armed Services Committee. As the newspaper *New York Times* reported on August 3, the CIA director described the Soviet military presence in the Indian Ocean as a relatively small one. In saying so he expressed the opinion that the final level of the Soviet forces in the Indian Ocean would depend on what forces the United States allotted for that area.[95]

---

91 A. A. Bessmenov, "The State Department," *SShA*, No. 10 (October 1970), pp. 104-11.

92 Yu. A. Shvedkov, "Reorganization of the National Security Council System," *SShA*, No. 2 (February 1970), pp. 112-16.

93 S. B. Chetverikov, " 'Organizational Problems' of Foreign Policy," *SShA,*

94 B. G. Rodanov and Yu. A. Yudin, "The CIA under the Fire of Criticism," *SShA*, No. 8 (August 1973), pp. 82-84, and A. N. Bandura, review article, in *SShA*, No. 4 (April 1974), pp. 104-04, on Ye. Ya. Yakovlev, *Sekrety sekretnykh sluzhb SShA* (Secrets of the U.S. Secret Services).

95 Moscow Tass release in English, August 31, 1974; cf. Moscow, Tass release in English, September 7, 1974.

Soviet analysts saw the CIA as opposing the Department of Defense on this issue, however temporarily, and advocating policies less hostile to the Soviet Union. While the full ramifications of this conflict within the U.S. foreign policy apparatus have not been discussed in Soviet media, they may be implicitly reflected in recent Russian suggestions that the military-industrial complex itself is divided into various factions.[96]

Soviet writers detect a serious factional split within another sector of the American foreign policy establishment: the community of researchers and scholars who analyze national strategy. Soviet respect for the influence of these defense analysts appears high; careful attention has been paid to the work of the Hudson Institute, Rand, the Brookings Institution, the Institute for Defense Analyses, MITRE, Stanford Research Institute and others.[97] Soviet observers, however, are well aware that the "think tanks" and strategists outside the government may differ significantly in their views. An entire article was devoted to the Arthur D. Little organization, whose director, General Gavin, had criticized Nixon's policy in Vietnam and earlier had opposed the policy of massive retaliation.[98] An even more laudatory article concerned the Center for Defense Information, whose "antimilitarist trend" and attacks on the B-1 bomber and Trident submarine programs were described as winning support from broad sectors of the American people, senators, scientists and public figures.[99]

---

[96] Reports of divergencies within the U.S. "military-industrial complex," such as between the DOD and CIA, are quite common in U.S. opinion media, which Soviet analysts follow closely and quote frequently. While Soviet party and military writers tend to emphasize the cohesiveness of the "military-industrial complex," more detailed analyses describe the divisions within this group, citing U.S. sources (most notably the Pentagon Papers) as evidence. See Shvedkov, *USA: The Foreign Policy Mechanism*, pp. 133-86.

[97] Cf. A. A. Topornin, "The Balance of Power Doctrine and Washington," *SShA*, No. 11 (November 1970), pp. 8-20, and V. V. Zhurkin, in a symposium at the Institute for the Study of the United States and Canada, *SShA*, No. 4 (April 1970), pp. 11-48, for the role of U.S. universities and research corporations in elaborating the methodology of U.S. foreign policy. Also I. L. Sheydina, *SShA: Fabriki mysli na sluzhbe strategii* (USA: "Think Tanks" in the Service of Strategy) (Moscow: "Nauka," 1973).

[98] Yu. Fel'chukov, "The Idea Factory," *SShA*, No. 3 (March 1970), pp. 94-105.

[99] B. D. Yashin, "The Center for Defense Information: Origins and Purposes," *SShA*, No. 6 (June 1973), pp. 63-66.

PRESIDENTIAL TRANSITION AND THE AMERICAN ELECTION PROCESS

One factor which has been understated in Soviet statements on the American foreign policy organization is the impact of the transition from President Nixon to President Ford. From the first month of the Ford administration, Soviet analysts saw no reason to change their views of American foreign policy, although Ford was described as having inherited a rather weak political base.

> After the first major steps toward normalizing Soviet-American relations were carried out by the Administration with the approval of the ruling class as a whole, there occurred what might be described as a "disintegration" of interests representing various political groups in the United States. "All right, now that we have a détente, what else do we need?" proclaimed numerous representatives of the American elite. The danger of war has been eliminated, they argued, and so now it should be possible to pursue again their private, petty and group interests—and even criticize those who persist in following the former line.[100]

Soviet analysts greeted the new President's promises of consistency in foreign policy with considerable warmth:

> The White House carries great weight in the shaping of U.S. foreign policy. Even now the new President has already made a number of statements touching on foreign policy problems, and broad circles of the world public have given a positive welcome to G. Ford's promise to maintain the U.S. foreign policy line, particularly in relations with the Soviet Union.[101]

Thus the initial Soviet view of President Ford consisted of two elements: (1) his actual power was seen as less than President Nixon enjoyed from 1969 to 1973, thanks to the growing strength of the Congress; but (2) his foreign policy was regarded as predicated on a definition of détente which did not violate Moscow's interests and intentions for Soviet-American relations.

As the time approached for the 1976 presidential election, however, new factors appeared which complicated the situation and the

---

[100] G. A. Trofimenko, "Problems of Peace and Security in Soviet-American Relations," *SShA*, No. 9 (September 1974), pp. 17-18.

[101] *Izvestiya*, September 3, 1974.

Soviet perceptions of the relationship between the two superpowers. Soviet analysts and commentators showed a keen interest in the primary election process.

In general, much of the commentary on the 1976 U.S. primary elections appeared in the major organs of the Soviet press, reporting results in a simple and factual manner. This is not surprising, since these articles were regularly based on materials and information available in Western sources. The more interpretive treatments, often exhibiting a high propaganda content, tended to be found in radio broadcasts and literature translated into foreign languages destined for external audiences.

The central issue of the primary campaign, which provoked Russian comment, concerned the future of Soviet-American relations— in particular, the issue of détente. A fundamental Soviet argument, reiterated constantly in their press, was that there is no alternative to détente:

> The debate about détente is not a matter of quibbling over terms. What is involved is the present and the future of international relations, a question of war and peace. Détente is indivisible, it is the same for the East and for the West. It is not advantageous to some and disadvantageous to others. Détente means the same thing for all. Only it must be understood correctly, realistically. If this is done there will be no exaggerated hopes and no unnecessary disenchantment.[102]

When on March 1, 1976, President Ford stated in an interview that he would no longer use the term "détente," but would substitute "peace through strength"[103] the initial Soviet comment included the observation that this might reflect tactical election considerations, but

> . . . sober-thinking commentators are not inclined to dramatize what the President said in his televised interview. The fact that he is not going to use a certain word does not yet mean he is surrendering a policy. . . . No, the word "détente" cannot be expunged from the world's political glossary. Even by a President.[104]

The general formulation advanced by Moscow in that period was

---

102 Editorial, "No Alternative to Détente," *New Times*, No. 12 (March 1976), p. 1.
103 See the article by Murray Marder in the *Washington Post*, March 3, 1976.
104 V. Kuznetsov, "Not 'Only a Word,' " *New Times*, No. 11 (March 1976), p. 16.

that though "right-wing attacks" on the policy of détente sometimes lead to a vacillation among the country's "ruling circles," caused by both tactical election considerations and dissatisfaction with the "misfortunes and failures of recent American policy," the later stages of the primary campaign would bring about a more realistic tone in statements on détente.[105]

The presidential contenders who in early 1976 received the most constant and heavy criticism in the Soviet press, Ronald Reagan and Henry Jackson, were identified as "enemies of détente" and "reactionaries." Moscow propagandists went to some lengths in their efforts to vilify these individuals. Categorized as a "bellicose figure" of the West, Reagan elicited harsh judgments:

> It begins to seem as if you are watching a screen on which they are showing an old grade-B cowboy movie. The Hollywood actor Ronald Reagan at one time appeared with pleasure in such films. He is now aspiring to the role of candidate for the presidency of the United States: A big strong guy bursts into the saloon with two pistols in his belt, throws dice or deals the cards, playing poker, but if there is no winning—bang-bang, bang, bang—and everything goes up in smoke. The main thing is force![106]

Reagan was further chastised for "deliberately distorting" the concept of détente in his attacks on administration policy. Refuting the idea that détente is a "one-way street" to the advantage of the Soviet Union, one Moscow commentator buttressed his counterargument with references to President Ford and Chancellor Schmidt and concluded:

> . . . It is at the very least absurd to demand from the Soviet Union a renunciation of its principled political line "in exchange for détente." This is clear to sober-minded politicians.
>
> Attention should be drawn to the fact that not one of the highest leaders of the chief states of the capitalist world has spoken publicly against the relaxation of tension. This can be regarded as the result of political realism and at the same time recognition of the fact that détente is supported by most people (and consequently most voters) in these states.[107]

---

[105] Yu. Babich, *Trud,* April 20, 1976, p. 1.

[106] Yu. Zhukov, "An Old-Fashioned Game," *Pravda,* April 8, 1976, p. 4.

[107] K. Karagezyan, "Common Sense and the Professional Scaremongers," *Za Rubezhom* (Abroad), No. 15 (April 9-15, 1976), p. 3.

A long-time target of Soviet abuse, Senator Henry Jackson inspired gleeful commentary from Moscow when he retired from active campaigning in April 1976. Soviet observers asserted that the reason for his lack of success with the American voters was his criticism of détente and the course of U.S.-Soviet relations:

> What reasons underlie this man's obvious lack of popularity with the voters? That is what some analysts are asking, and they tend to furnish such answers as the Senator's lack of charisma, his plodding oratory style. . . .
> The reasons for Henry Jackson's fiasco, and I don't think you can call it anything else, are quite evident. All you have to do is open your eyes. The Senator from Boeing has consistently spoken out against better Soviet-U.S. relations, against relaxation of international tension.[108]

Senator Jackson's support of Israel has long provoked vituperative criticism from Soviet writers, and Moscow portrayed him as the favorite of U.S. Zionism in the primary campaign. Jackson's appeal to the American Jewish community, strengthened by the enlistment of that "notorious advocate of Zionism," Daniel Moynihan, was described in the remarks of a Soviet press correspondent:

> . . . financially he is way ahead of his rivals. Speaking in synagogues across the country, he heaps abuse on Middle East Arab states, flatters Tel Aviv, promising Israel unlimited military aid if returned, and vilifies Moscow at the same time.[109]

The Soviets charged that Jackson's effort to link the granting of most-favored-nation status for the Soviet Union and the provision of credits by the Export-Import Bank to the liberalization of Soviet emigration policy aided no one. The Soviet Union refused to "buckle to his demands" and its emigration policy has remained the same. Furthermore, Jackson's anti-Soviet activities were alleged to have had negative repercussions for American business. According to one Moscow commentator, "U.S. companies, frustrated by Jackson's activity, are doing business with the Soviet Union through foreign affiliates, thus taking away jobs from tens of thousands of Americans," and "the Soviet Union has turned to Western European

---

108 Commentary by Vladimir Pozner, Radio Moscow, May 3, 1976.
109 Iona Andronov, "At the Distant Approaches to the White House," *New Times*, No. 12 (March 1976), p. 10.

and Japanese companies, striking mutually profitable bargains with them, bargains that could have been made with U.S. companies."[110] The propagandistic character of this argument becomes evident when the practical realities of Soviet-American trade are considered. Even had the Jackson-Vanik Amendment not been adopted, the United States would not have offered trade terms equivalent to those available in Western Europe.

It is evident that the chronic hard-currency problems of the Soviet Union, coupled with recent disastrous crop failures and a decline in the prices of major Soviet export commodities, are dictating the limits to the current program of technology imports by the USSR. Because U.S. recovery from the severe recession appeared rapid and relatively assured, pressure for the provision of government-backed credits to the USSR was not as intense as in Western Europe. Thus, rather than joining in any backlash against Senator Jackson, many American businessmen adopted this more realistic view of the potential for trade with the Soviet Union, although this view has of course not been shared by the more vocal proponents of expanded Soviet-American trade.

Soviet commentaries alleged that the Pentagon plays a major role in the primary campaign, as an integral part of the "group" which Moscow subsumes under the rubric of "enemies of détente." This group was described as

> ... an alliance of military industrialists, fanatical militarists, pathological anti-Communists and reactionaries of every stripe. It is not a large group in number but it controls entire propaganda concerns which use the most subtle tricks to dislodge the masses from common-sense positions and convince them of the "danger" of détente.[111]

Moscow asserted that high-ranking military officers and defense officials "constantly supply reactionary aspirants for the presidency with electioneering 'arguments.' " The Pentagon was cited as the source of numerous tales about "the 'growth of the Soviet military budget,' the 'Soviet military and political expansion,' etc."[112]

In addition to the alleged role played by the Pentagon, the Rus-

---

[110] Pozner, Radio Moscow, May 3, 1976.
[111] Karagezyan, *op. cit.*, p. 3.
[112] Tass release, "Zigzags of the U.S. Election Campaign," April 13, 1976.

sians argued that the "reactionary" candidates (Reagan and Jackson) were also advised and aided by a "new brain trust," which appeared at the beginning of the campaign.

> The "brain trust" recommendations are being widely used in their election campaigns by Jackson and Reagan, who are working hard to carry them to as large a number of voters as possible.[113]

The Soviets portrayed this "brain trust" as an "ideological base for the offensive against détente," and described it thus:

> It was set up on the basis of the Johns Hopkins University School of Advanced International Studies, where none other than ex-Defense Secretary James Schlesinger is now ensconced, and the Center for Strategic and International Studies at Georgetown University, which is headed by Schlesinger's one-time CIA colleague and former head of intelligence at the State Department, Ray Cline, who resigned from his State Department post because of disagreement with U.S. policy toward the Soviet Union.[114]

As the primary campaign progressed, Moscow saw as arrayed against these "reactionary" forces and candidates the more "soberminded" politicians, among them Governor James Carter, Senators Hubert Humphrey and Edward Kennedy, and Congressman Morris Udall. While their comments regarding these candidates who seemed somewhat less objectionable to Moscow were relatively restrained, the overall pattern regarding the U.S. election process is clearly one of keen Soviet interest. Also, there would seem to be no inhibitions on Moscow's part against influencing the process, if by any means the wielding of such influence were made possible, since the identity of the next occupant of the White House was obviously a matter of vital interest to the Kremlin.

Implications of Soviet Views

In assessing the overall strengths and weaknesses of the United States, Soviet observers employ both absolute and relativistic analyses. In absolute terms, American military and technological capabilities are seen as enormous and growing. The current U.S. economic

---

[113] Nikolai Turkatenko, "The Presidential Marathon," *New Times*, No. 18 (April 1976), p. 23.
[114] *Ibid.*

crisis is viewed as serious but not imminently fatal, since the fundamental economic base is sound. In relative terms, however, compared with the USSR, the United States is perceived as becoming increasingly weak. As the director of the Institute for the Study of the United States and Canada has said, "International events of recent times indicated . . . the radical difference between socialism and imperialism in the political utilization of increased power."[115] It is the inherent nature of the capitalist sociopolitical system which is said to preclude successful "political utilization" of U.S. power in competition with the USSR.

The propositions which form the core of the Soviet analysis of American society and government are (1) that the U.S. sociopolitical system is weakened and divded by irreconcilable conflicts between the social classes and within the bourgeoisie itself; (2) that U.S. foreign policy is frequently unpredictable, because of the shifting allegiances of those few individuals or groups which have the power to make decisions which favor their private interests over the needs of U.S. society as a whole; and (3) that the economic and political crises which have emerged in the United States, as well as the failures of U.S. foreign policy due to the shift which has taken place in the correlation of world forces, have contributed to a weakening of the American national will, among both the leadership and society.

Although Soviet propaganda belabors the alleged irrationality, exploitation and aimlessness of the capitalist system, it is the perception of internal conflict which seems most central in shaping Soviet behavior toward the United States.

Soviet observers see the United States as unable to manage economic growth and social evolution, let alone to understand and incorporate the true fruits of the scientific-technological revolution. By virtue of its very institutional and organizational structure, the capitalist economy is depicted as incapable of fulfilling national tasks and meeting international challenges in a changing world environment. Soviet spokesmen contend that internal conflict, irrationality and exploitation will eventually cause a revolutionary change in the American system, but for the near future they seem to anticipate continuing Soviet competition with a viable imperialist government.

---

115 Arbatov, "An Event of World Significance," *op. cit.*, p. 9.

American
Military Power Appraised

I T HAS OFTEN been remarked that Lenin was fascinated by military science and history and that Leninism-Stalinism is permeated by military terms and concepts. Notions of struggle, conflict and war abound; the use of force to achieve political ends is one of the core principles of the Soviet belief system. It is not surprising, therefore, that Soviet perceptions of the military power of the United States are an essential element in their ongoing assessment of the competition between two world systems. This assessment, informed by estimates of U.S. military capabilities and the resolve of the United States to employ them in the pursuit of national goals, is a fundamental consideration in the formulation and implementation of Soviet foreign policy.

Soviet analysts propound a decisive shift in the world correlation of forces in favor of socialism. Under the conditions of strategic parity and in the atmosphere of "détente," Soviet spokesmen have argued that the role of nonmilitary factors is enhanced, so that political, economic, social, ideological and scientific-technological issues assume a new prominence in the course of world development and international relations. It is important to recognize, however, that the extent to which this is true stems largely from the immense and growing military capabilities of the USSR, which have heightened the risks associated with the use of force by the United States in regions where the interests of the two superpowers are in sharp conflict. Thus the military relationship is fundamental; it affects all aspects and the entire range of superpower competition.

In consigning a critical role to military factors, Soviet spokesmen

are explicit in drawing a distinction between the purposes of the
armed forces of the Soviet Union and those of the United States.

> The military potential of the two opposed systems also has a great
> effect on the real balance of forces in the world. Here it is neces-
> sary to take into account that the destination of these military po-
> tentials is fundamentally opposed. . . . The defensive might of the
> Soviet Union ensures peaceful communist construction in our
> country . . . and does not threaten other peoples. The military
> might of the USA has another meaning. Imperialism . . . is inter-
> ested in solving important social problems by war. . . . The military
> potential of the imperialist states includes the threat of war.[1]

Soviet military might, however, is seen as useful for many purposes in addition to those of deterrence and fighting wars. Especially important are the perceived political utilities of military
power; in fact, "the invincible might of the Soviet Army and Navy
. . . [is] one of the most important factors in determining the role and
influence of the Soviet state in the world arena."[2] Soviet armed
forces constrain the aggressive designs of world imperialism, inhibit
the projection of U.S. power abroad and prevent America from
using military means to accomplish political goals. For these reasons, Soviet military power has advanced the cause of national liberation around the world.

> The colossal might of the Soviet Union . . . serves the just cause of
> the struggle against imperialist aggression and the suppression of
> peoples. . . . The growth of this might, as well as the greater influ-
> ence of the USSR on the course of events in the world, corresponds
> to the vital interests of the masses in all nations, and to the interests
> of the revolutionary and liberation movement of the working class
> and all working people.[3]

---

[1] Colonel S. Tyushkevich, Doctor of Philosophical Sciences, "The Balance of Forces
in the World and the Factors to Prevent War," *Kommunist Vooruzhennykh Sil*
(the journal of the Main Political Administration of the Soviet Army and Navy),
No. 10 (May 1974), pp. 10-16.

[2] Editorial article, "Role and Organization of the Soviet Armed Forces: Command,
Political and Engineering-Technical Personnel," *Kommunist Vooruzhennykh Sil*,
No. 18 (September 1972), pp. 21-22.

[3] Colonel General N. A. Lomov, ed., *Scientific-Technical Progress and the Revolution in Military Affairs* (A Soviet View) (Moscow, 1973); translated and published under the auspices of the U.S. Air Force (Washington, D.C.: U.S. Government Printing Office, 1974), p. 271.

Given the importance Soviet spokesmen attribute to military factors in the international political arena, it is not surprising that they devote much effort to assessing the military capabilities of their chief adversary, the United States. Soviet views about American military power reflect two broad themes. The first concerns the so-called class-based analysis (doctrinal appreciation) of the inherently aggressive nature and repressive sociopolitical function of the military in bourgeois capitalist states, as well as the more instrumental aspect of imperialist military-political blocs and alliance systems by which military power is marshaled and projected abroad. The second theme relates more directly to the operational capabilities of the armed forces, important aspects of which include human factors, deployed weapons systems or those under development, military budgeting and planning in the U.S. government and the main trends in American military strategy.

The above topics appear with great frequency in Soviet military and authoritative CPSU publications and reflect the perceptual framework through which the Soviets derive assessments of U.S. military power. These topics encompass a wide range of issues, including military-technical, political, economic and social-psychological factors, the sum of which are considered by the Soviets in assessing the military components of national power. As in their comprehensive and complex estimates of the world correlation of forces and the general strategic capabilities of the United States, Russian planners approach the problem of assessing the U.S. military with a holistic outlook. They conceive of the American defense establishment as an integral subsystem of the greater capitalist socioeconomic system, performing essential functions, and deriving its nature and identity from its relation to bourgeois capitalist society. By integrating a broad scope of factors, and viewing the military within its socioeconomic milieu, Soviet planners develop estimates of U.S. military capabilities, and appraise Washington's will and resolve to employ them in pursuit of national goals. Moscow's assessments focus on the "objective" character of the military under the conditions of state monopoly capitalism, the instrumental political-military blocs and cohesion among capitalist states, and operational capabilities of the armed forces, as well as the domestic and international constraints and weaknesses of a military, political, economic, social and psychological nature which curtail the effective use of military means by the United States.

Since the Soviet armed forces receive constant political indoctrination, it is not surprising that Russian commentary on the U.S. military approaches the subject from a Marxist-Leninist perspective. Soviet evaluations of the American military, therefore, differ from those which would be derived from non-Communist sources.

Role and Function of the Military in Capitalist States

Contemporary Marxist-Leninist teaching in the Soviet Union describes the military in capitalist societies as having two broad purposes, one internal, the other external:

> All bourgeois armies, irrespective of their social structure, serve as the principal means of asserting the . . . rule of the capitalists, as a means of suppressing the working people in the country and enslaving the peoples of other countries. Their internal and external functions are closely linked.[4]

According to this view, the internal role of an army is basically to function "as the internal prop of the capitalist system."[5] The standing army, therefore, is considered to be a reactionary weapon of the capitalists with which to suppress the workers and progressive movements, preserving the power of the ruling class.

The external function of the army within capitalist states is said not to be defensive, but rather to serve as the instrument for the monopoly-capitalist policy of annexation, expropriation and exploitation, carried out by means of the use or threat of force:

> Its main purpose is not to defend its own country but to attack other countries in order to rob and enslave the working people. Defense is only derivative of the universal striving of the exploiters after attack. The weaker states, falling victim to aggression by a strong predator, are compelled to defend themselves.[6]

The deepening crisis of capitalism in its state monopoly stage and

---

[4] *Marxism-Leninism on War and the Army* (Moscow: Progress Publishers, 1972), p. 190.
[5] *Ibid.*
[6] *Ibid.*, p. 191.

the growing contradictions of capitalist society are seen by Moscow as spurring the United States into provocative, adventuristic and dangerous policies. Describing imperialism, or state monopoly capitalism in its highest stage, Marshal of the Soviet Union and Minister of Defense A. A. Grechko notes this increasingly aggressive posture:

> The weakening of the positions of imperialism and the capitalist system's feeling of doom intensify the aggressiveness and adventurism of reactionary-monopolistic circles. Here and there they provoke military conflicts, which are directed against the Soviet Union, the entire socialist community and the forces of national liberation.
>
> The militarists vainly attempt to overcome the insoluble internal social, economic and ideological contradictions of the capitalist system, to weaken the world socialist system and to deal with the international worker and national liberation movement by the path of political subversion, blackmail and aggressive wars.[7]

The Soviets perceive the "aggressive policies" and military capabilities of capitalism in general, and that of the United States in particular, to be directed at world socialism, whether it be the USSR, other socialist countries, national liberation movements abroad or revolutionary movements within capitalist states.

Alliances and Imperialist Blocs

One of the fundamental instruments to project American power abroad, in Moscow's view, is the system of "imperialist military-political blocs" or alliances. These alliances are described as characteristic formations occurring under the sociopolitical conditions of imperialism, the highest stage of capitalism:

> The appearance of military-political alliances, their social nature and the characteristics and specific features of their functioning are determined entirely by the needs of certain sociopolitical forces.

---

[7] A. A. Grechko, *Vooruzhennyye Sily Sovetskogo gosudarstva* (Moscow: Voyenizdat, 1974), p. 401. See also Colonel General P. Gorchakov, chief of the Soviet Strategic Missile Forces Political Directorate, "Paths of Glory," *Sovetskaya Kultura* (Soviet Culture), February 21, 1975, p. 1.

The Atlantic ideologists conceal this truth. Using artificially con-
trived conceptions of the origin of military coalitions, they attempt
to remove the blame for the arms race from imperialism.[8]

Soviet writers identify as typical features the militarism, "class
nature" and anti-socialist orientation of these alliances:

> In many capitalist countries the growth of state monopoly capital-
> ism is pervasively accompanied by a growth of militarism. The
> imperialist war machine, directed primarily against the socialist
> states, is designed to preserve and strengthen the exploiting system.
> . . . Governments of NATO countries have been emphasizing war
> preparations ever since that aggressive bloc was formed.[9]

Their principal goal is alleged to be that of "maintaining and
strengthening the system of capitalist exploitation and oppression."[10]
Despite the current atmosphere of relaxed tension between states
having different social systems, the existence of aggressive and dangerous capitalist military-political blocs is seen by the Soviets as
requiring "constant vigilance":

> In the capitalist world, the positions of the reactionary forces are
> still quite strong. . . . [There] is the unceasing and active work
> being carried out by the imperialist military-political blocs. . . .
> The headquarters of these blocs continue to develop military plans
> and measures for intensifying the arms race and . . . for carrying out
> combat operations against the socialist countries.[11]

Of the various capitalist military alliances of which the United
States is a primary member, NATO has received the most attention
in the Soviet press. It has been subject to intense propaganda as well
as informed analysis in the diverse academic, party and military
publications of the USSR. According to the Kremlin, NATO is
foremost among capitalist military alliances in terms of its formidable power, its resources and its threat to socialism and all progressive movements:

---

[8] Colonel V. Rodin, Doctor of Philosophical Sciences, "The Ideology of Atlanticism
in the Service of the Enemies of Détente," *Kommunist Vooruzhennykh Sil*, No. 19
(October 1974), p. 26.
[9] Unsigned article, "Imperialism's Powder Kegs," *World Marxist Review*, XVIII,
No. 4 (April 1975), 38.
[10] Colonel V. Katerinich, "NATO, SEATO, and CENTO . . . Composition and
Aims," *Bloknot Agitatora*, No. 15 (August 1973), in JPRS 60087, *Translations on
USSR Military Affairs*, No. 959 (September 20, 1973), p. 10.
[11] *Ibid.*, p. 9.

In the aggressive plans of the militaristic circles of the West, a special role is played by the main imperialist military bloc—NATO. It is the largest and most organized military-political grouping of the capitalist states . . . in terms of its area, the populations involved, the production of the principal types of industrial products and the size of its armed forces, the North Atlantic Treaty Organization does not have an equal among the other imperialist military blocs. The entire nuclear potential of the capitalist world is concentrated in the NATO countries.[12]

NATO is not viewed as limiting its activity to Western Europe. Rather, NATO is portrayed as the "spearhead of the imperialists" for the struggle against democratic and national liberation movements throughout the world.[13] As evidence of this, Soviet authors cite NATO support and assistance "to the Israeli extremists who are continuing their aggressive actions against the Arab countries," and in the past, to the "Portuguese colonists waging a bloody war against the patriots of Guinea, Angola and Mozambique," and the expansion of U.S. and NATO forces deployed in the Indian Ocean.[14] Despite the assertion of a worldwide role for NATO, it is NATO's basically European focus and direction, however, which commands most Soviet attention. Claiming that the Western European countries are being transformed into "military bridgeheads" complete with numerous headquarters, troop concentrations, stockpiles of ammunition and fuel, a dense network of airfields and a combined armed forces created under a unified command,[15] Soviet authors note:

> . . . it is readily apparent that Western Europe is the principal zone of activity for NATO, selected by imperialism to serve as the main bridgehead. It is precisely in this region that two world wars have been unleashed, with many millions of human lives being lost. It is here that one finds the line of direct contact between the European socialist countries and the world of imperialism.[16]

---

12 Lieutenant General A. M. Shevchenko, gen. ed., *Armii Stran NATO* (Armies of the NATO Countries) (Moscow: Voyennoye Izdatelstvo, 1974). Excerpts translated in JPRS 63989, *Translations on USSR Military Affairs*, No. 1114 (January 20, 1975), p. 37.
13 *Ibid.*
14 Katerinich, *op. cit.*, pp. 9-10.
15 *Ibid.*, p. 11.
16 Shevchenko, *op. cit.*, p. 37.

In addition to the land mass of Western Europe, Russian analysts recognize the Mediterranean as occupying an important strategic position, in which "military-strategic factors play a tremendous role."[17] They have noted that the NATO command maintains in the Southern European Theater combined armed forces including large numbers of ground forces, naval and air forces, as well as the main striking force in the theater, the 16th Squadron of U.S. Polaris submarines and the Sixth Fleet. One Soviet author describes the role of these NATO forces as follows:

> NATO's domination in the southeastern part of the theater of military operations [the territories of Greece and Turkey and adjacent areas of the sea] makes it possible, the NATO leaders consider, to control the sea routes leading from the Black Sea to the Mediterranean and the area of the Black Sea straits, to threaten the left flank of the Warsaw Pact nations and the Arab states in the Near and Middle East, and in case of outbreak of war, to deliver nuclear strikes against military and industrial targets in the USSR and other socialist nations.[18]

The author goes on to couple the NATO Southern European theater of operations directly with imperialism's global strategic interests in the region. Specifically, the Mediterranean-Southern European region "is assigned the role of a link between the Atlantic and the Indian Ocean, calculated to ensure control over the oil resources of the Arabian Peninsula and the Persian Gulf."[19] Moreover, in the Soviet view, the power of U.S. forces abroad is considerably enhanced by the deployment of forward-based systems (FBS). The Soviets define FBS to include any non-central-U.S. nuclear delivery system capable of striking the territory of the USSR. This definition then encompasses American strike aircraft and Pershing missiles deployed in Europe as well as carrier-based aircraft deployed in the Mediterranean, Western Pacific and Indian Ocean. A Moscow Radio commentator's remarks on September 17, 1974, illustrate the Soviet position:

> . . . there are some 650 aircraft at bases in Europe and Asia and on

---

[17] Colonel K. Kozlov, "The Mediterranean and NATO," *Kommunist Vooruzhennykh Sil,* No. 12 (June 1975), p .71.
[18] *Ibid.*
[19] *Ibid.*

the United States aircraft carriers that are capable of delivering nuclear weapons to Soviet territory. Moreover, the United States, unlike the Soviet Union, has advanced bases for its submarines. Also the United States troops in Federal Germany are reported to have more than 7000 nuclear weapons for tactical missiles whose radius of action extends over a large part of the Soviet Union. So, are they tactical or strategic weapons, these nuclear devices based close to the Soviet Union? I would call them strategic.

Consistent with these views, CPSU General Secretary Leonid Brezhnev advanced a proposal in his Warsaw address of July 21, 1974, to negotiate on the removal from the Mediterranean of all Soviet and American ships and submarines bearing nuclear weapons.[20] Emphasizing the importance the USSR attaches to this, just prior to the Vladivostok summit meeting, President of the USSR Supreme Soviet and Politburo member N. V. Podgorny, in Sofia, Bulgaria, delivered a speech again calling for the denuclearization of the Mediterranean:

> The Soviet Union advocates making the Mediterranean a zone free from nuclear weapons, a zone of peace. This would be facilitated by a withdrawal from the region of the Mediterranean Sea of ships with nuclear weapons on board. The Soviet Union will carry out this important step but, of course, on the basis of reciprocity.[21]

Another theater of operations in which U.S. and NATO country activity receives continuing attention in the Soviet press is the Indian Ocean-Persian Gulf region. This area, it is alleged, is seen by NATO imperialists as important for their strategic designs against the USSR as well as their efforts to constrain national liberation movements. Soviet military analysts and political commentators have noted an increasing interest on the part of the United States and members of NATO in building up forces deployed there and developing strategic capabilities through the expansion of base facilities for both air and naval elements:

In the opinion of the foreign political analysts and military experts,

---

20 Brezhnev speech before Polish Sejm, July 21, 1974, cited in *FBIS*, "Daily Report—Soviet Union," July 22, 1974, p. D-14.
21 Podgorny speech at Sofia, Bulgaria, September 8, 1974, cited in *FBIS*, "Daily Report—Soviet Union," September 9, 1974, p. D-7. See also Admiral Gorshkov, *Pravda*, July 28, 1974.

the Indian Ocean and the countries adjacent to it are now regarded as a gradually emerging independent geopolitical complex. The significance of the Indian Ocean itself as a theater of military operations is increasing. The attention of imperialist strategists, and particularly aggressive American circles, has been attracted to its northern areas which lie near the USSR . . . [for the purpose] of supporting naval strike forces—aircraft-carrier large units and atomic missile submarines . . .[22]

The aggressive intentions of the Western powers are indicated by the fact that the North Atlantic Assembly "has insisted that the West maintain a permanent naval presence in the Indian Ocean."[23] Furthermore, the "high command of the naval forces of the United States and several other NATO countries . . . [uses] the bases and ports of Pakistan, Indonesia, Iran, the Republic of South Africa and Sri Lanka."[24] The issue of bases is viewed by the Soviets as fundamental to Western strategy vis-à-vis the USSR, the socialist nations and the Third World in general. The system of bases in the Indian Ocean facilitates "imperialist" control of the region, restrains national liberation movements through the show or use of force and continues the "rapacious extraction" by "American and other Western monopolies" of the region's vital natural resources. Finally, the network of bases and the deployment of Western forces in the Indian Ocean are viewed as an integral part of the global strategy of imperialism:

> The network of bases in the Indian Ocean cannot be regarded as an isolated case. It is an integral part of the imperialist powers' unified "base" system, and its aim is to unify their "military presence" in two other regions of the world—the Atlantic and the Pacific. This is necessary for them so that they can increase the opportunities of broad maneuver by the armed forces, the rapid transfer of these forces from one ocean to another and the buildup in concentration of forces in any particular region in order to exert pressure on the independent states of Africa and South and Southeast Asia.[25]

---

[22] Captain 1st Rank K. Titov, "The Indian Ocean on the Charts of the Pentagon," *Morskoy Sbornik* (Naval Digest), No. 7 (July 1973), p. 92. Captain Titov is a Doctor of Naval Sciences and professor.

[23] Captain 2nd Rank G. Melkov, "The Sources of Tension," *Krasnaya Zvezda*, June 9, 1974.

[24] Titov, *op. cit.*, p. 93.

[25] Melkov, *op. cit.*

According to Moscow, the semicircle of Anglo-American military bases which extends from South Africa north to the Persian Gulf and southeast to Australia will comprise a "strategic triangle" once the expansion of Diego Garcia is completed. The facilities at Diego Garcia are viewed as an important "strong point" in this chain of bases:

> Diego Garcia occupies a special place in it. The reequipping of the base on this island will eventually cost 75 million. . . . Even now everyone knows that this base is to be used to service B-52 strategic bombers and ships of all classes, including assault aircraft carriers and nuclear missile submarines. According to Admiral Zumwalt, U.S. Navy Chief of Staff, the Diego Garcia naval and air base "will enable the United States to deploy armed forces in the Indian Ocean region and thus to maintain the American foreign policy course maintained there."[26]

In the Soviet view, U.S. and NATO bases in the Atlantic, the Mediterranean, the Indian Ocean and the Pacific are to be considered an important component of the military power of imperialism, in that they support forward-based systems, air, ground and naval forces, which may be projected abroad, far from the shores of the United States or Western Europe. These forces serve a dual function: they are alert and ready to execute a retaliatory nuclear strike upon the Soviet Union and its allies in the event of superpower war; and they are being used as a means of political "persuasion" or military coercion over local regional states. Such capabilities grant the United States a certain measure of freedom to maneuver in world politics and offer U.S. decisionmakers a range of military-political options which they would not enjoy in the absence of such coercive diplomacy.

Constraints on U.S. Military Power

Military alliances such as NATO, with its far-flung system of air and naval bases from which military power may be projected abroad, are still considered by the Soviets to constitute a formidable threat. They have noted, however, that the trend toward relaxation

---

[26] *Ibid.*

of international tension, resulting from the shift in the correlation of forces, has heightened inherent contradictions within NATO. The new era of détente and peaceful coexistence, for example, has exacerbated conflicts between the United States and its NATO allies, by bringing into question the two fundamental principles maintaining NATO solidarity—"anti-communism" and the appreciation of mutual economic benefits stemming from close U.S.-Western European ties.[27] Peaceful coexistence, Soviet spokesmen argue, undermined the ideological principle of anti-communism and thus deprived NATO of its "omnipotent and cementing element."[28] In the words of a Soviet military analyst, the world relaxation of tensions culminating in détente "destroyed the foundation on which the North Atlantic Alliance rests."[29] The general effect of all this has been internal political changes in member states and a softening of NATO's posture:

> A manifestation of this positive process is the consolidation of the positions of the more moderate wing in the ruling quarters of capitalist states, including member countries of the North Atlantic Alliance. Realistic considerations incline its spokesmen not to obstruct détente, to lower somewhat NATO's military activity and to look for peaceful solutions of urgent international issues.[30]

The belief that NATO would bring mutual U.S.-Western European economic benefits, which Moscow says is the other fundamental principle that in the past operated to maintain NATO solidarity, is no longer strongly held among the European allies. A series of conflicts and contradictions have eroded this principle:

> Conflicts within the framework of NATO . . . are primarily contradictions of a military-economic nature. The . . ."Common Market" . . . has become a strong economic competitor of the USA. The trend of a number of NATO nations to withdraw from the military organization of that bloc, following France's example, is manifesting itself more and more persistently. The government of Greece,

---

27 A. I. Utkin, "Atlanticism vs. Europeism: Struggle of Conceptions," *SShA*, No. 4 (April 1974), p. 4.
28 *Ibid.*, p. 29.
29 Lieutenant Colonel G. Sokov'yev, "NATO Generals Are True to Themselves," *Voyennyye Znaniye,* No. 1 (January 1974), p. 42.
30 A. Antonov, "NATO and Détente," *Soviet Military Review*, No. 6 (June 1974), p. 56.

for example, has announced its decision to leave the North Atlantic Treaty Organization. Certain NATO states are attempting to reduce their military allocations.[31]

NATO, according to Soviet observers, is increasingly developing centrifugal tendencies.[32] These tendencies were dramatically manifest during the 1973 Middle East war and subsequent oil embargo. The oil crisis, the Soviets assert, has played an instrumental role in aggravating the already poor relations between the capitalist powers.[33] The independent position taken by most of the NATO countries and Japan during the October War, as well as their expressed displeasure over Washington's use of bases on their soil to aid Israel, was noted by Soviet commentators:

> The world is witnessing a sharp exacerbation of contradictions—economic, political and military—between the United States of America and Western European NATO allies. To the discontent of the latter over Washington's unilateral actions during the military conflict in the Middle East in October 1973 have been added sharp differences over the ways of overcoming the energy crisis and over the policy toward countries of the Arab East.[34]

Soviet observers allege that NATO is not the only Western military alliance to be undergoing the process of political decay and disintegration. In the case of SEATO, the alliance's decay and dissolution are ascribed to the "defeat" of the United States in Indochina. Putting forward a Moscow version of the domino theory, Soviet commentators claim that the lost war in Vietnam spawned a political reorientation among member Asian states, making SEATO an "anachronism":

> Both the aggravation of internal contradictions between the members of the bloc and the social changes which found expression in a new foreign political orientation of a number of member countries made for its final disintegration. Attempts to prevent the failure of

---

31 Colonel V. Rodin, "Some Questions on the Origin and Development of Military Alliances," *Voyenno-Istoricheskiy Zhurnal*, No. 2 (February 1975), p. 87.

32 Colonel V. Rodin, "The Ideology of Atlanticism in the Service of the Enemies of Détente," *Kommunist Vooruzhennykh*, No. 19 (October 1974), p. 22.

33 R. Andreasyan, "Oil and the Anti-Imperialist Struggle," *Kommunist* No. 5 (March 1974), p. 107. See also N. N. Inozemtsev, "Capitalism of the 70s: The Aggravation of Contradictions," *Pravda*, August 20, 1974.

34 Antonov, *op. cit.*, p. 56.

SEATO continued until the last minute but the positive changes in the world arena cut the ground from beneath the feet of its supporters.[35]

Along with the political decay of Western alliance systems and the heightened contradictions of capitalism, the Soviets identify other elements which have combined to constrain the projection and use of military force by the United States. Perhaps the most important of these are the increased military capabilities of the USSR, which may be employed to "neutralize" or inhibit the use of force by the United States and its allies, thus providing a "shield" for the national liberation struggle. According to the Soviet formulation, national liberation wars may occur either within states or between states. Specifically, national liberation struggles within states occur between the "oppressed" classes and the "oppressor" class; national liberation struggles carried out between states are those which the Soviets have classified as "anti-imperialist" in character, aimed at the "neocolonialist," exploitative policies of capitalist states. Successful national liberation movements, in the Soviet view, weaken the American position in the world generally and may result in denying the United States access to strategic areas and bases. The Soviet military is seen as playing an important role in facilitating the national liberation struggle, and preventing Western intervention:

> One cannot fail to see that the military might of the socialist community serves as an obstacle to the export of counterrevolution by the imperialists and thus *objectively promotes the development of revolutionary and liberation movements*.[36]

Other constraints in the American military's use of force and projection of its power abroad have domestic origins. Taken together, these constraints constitute a lack of will on the part of Washington to support an activist foreign policy, prepared to employ military means when necessary, in order to achieve its aims. This lack of will may be observed in the American people's negative attitude toward the army, reduction of troops overseas and the termination of the

---

[35] Radio broadcast, Oleg Pleshkov commentator, Tass, Moscow, September 25, 1974, cited in *FBIS*, "Daily Report—Soviet Union," September 26, 1975, p. A-8.
[36] General of the Army A. A. Yepishev, "The Soviet Army's Historic Mission," *Soviet Military Review*, No. 2 (February 1974), p. 6. Emphasis in the original.

draft and its replacement by the all-volunteer force.[37] Soviet analysts claim that these things have occurred because of a trend in United States public opinion which they construe as "antimilitaristic." This trend rejects the use of vast expenditures to support military operations overseas to the detriment of domestic programs:

> A characteristic feature of the sociopolitical life of the United States of America in recent years has been the spread of antimilitarism. . . . The ruinous socioeconomic consequences of the colossal military expenditures and militaristic trends in American politics and economics have been revealed . . . the war in Vietnam and the sharpening of internal conflicts have generated a powerful wave of antiwar movement. They have intensified the dissatisfaction of many Americans with . . . political priorities oriented toward satisfying the . . . military-industrial complex at the expense of the urgent needs of the society.[38]

The public outcry against large expenditures for defense has echoed within the halls of Congress as well; the Soviets have noted that in recent years congressional "opposition to militarism has expanded significantly":

> In the highest legislative body of the United States, the political struggle with respect to various problems connected with financing military spending has intensified noticeably. The process of approving military estimates has become more complicated. Whereas in recent years this was essentially a formality and a brief procedure sometimes ending up even with the Pentagon receiving more than it had requested, now the situation has changed clearly not in favor of the military.[39]

Indeed, the opposition of the legislative branch to the military budget has not gone unnoticed even at the top level of the CPSU hierarchy. Boris Ponomarev, candidate member of the Politburo and a secretary of the Central Committee of the CPSU, speaking to a delegation of the U.S. House of Representatives in August 1975,

---

[37] A. Trofimenko, "On U.S. Military-Political Strategies," *SShA*, No. 12 (December 1971), pp. 3-4.

[38] N. A. Dolgopolova, "Military Spending and Public Opinion," *SShA*, No. 2 (February 1975), p. 114. See also G. A. Arbatov, "U.S. Foreign Policy and the Scientific and Technical Revolution," *SShA*, No. 10 (October 1973), p. 9.

[39] *Ibid.*

attacked the size of the American defense budget, but praised the efforts of the Congress to hold down military spending:

> We note that recently the role of the House of Representatives in the decision of questions of foreign policy has been wholly outstanding, and we are convinced that its members can do much to stop the outbreak of a new round of the arms race.[40]

Actions of the Congress, such as cutting significantly the military appropriations for the 1976 fiscal year, may be attributed, said Tass on September 25, 1975, to "the pressure of public opinion—an overwhelming majority of Americans firmly come out against a further increase in military spending . . ." While Congress as a whole is viewed as becoming more hostile to defense spending, Soviet spokesmen see the Senate as especially opposed to the Pentagon's money requests. This is attributed to the "relatively skeptical attitude of a certain group of senators toward the need to expand military programs at a time of emerging relaxation of tension," and their need to take into account "purely domestic economic factors, primarily inflation."[41]

The trend toward reducing or limiting the defense budget in the United States is viewed as accelerating similar trends in the NATO countries:

> Under conditions of economic disorders, the United States' NATO allies are finding it increasingly difficult to finance the big orders of their defense ministers. A trend toward limiting military budgets has begun to be observed in a number of Western European countries—a fact which James Schlesinger, U.S. Secretary of Defense, was informed of during his recently concluded visit to Western Europe. In this sense the results of the vote in the House of Representatives may indirectly prompt certain NATO countries to implement their plans to cut their military programs.[42]

Defense spending as a major point of conflict between the legislative and executive branches of the U.S. government is a growing theme in the Soviet press. With regard to the procedural mechanism

---

[40] *Washington Post*, August 12, 1975, p. A-14. See also *Pravda*, August 24, 1974, p. 5.
[41] A. Artamonov, "The Pentagon Is Extorting . . . ," *Izvestiya*, October 8, 1975, morning edition.
[42] *Ibid.*

of the Planning, Programming, Budgeting System of the Defense Department, one Soviet author asserts that major obstacles of an organizational and political variety impede efforts at increasing the viability of the system, and notes the role of the legislative branch:

> Among the latter, in particular, is the interdepartmental rivalry in the Pentagon for gaining a predominant position in the military planning and budgeting system, as well as the contradictions between the executive bodies and legislative power. The acute and protracted political struggle which has arisen in the ruling upper clique of the United States in the process of drawing up the budget is the main cause for serious disruptions in the rhythmical functioning of the PPB system's procedural mechanism.[43]

Soviet commentators have responded to other indications that might spell constraints on the global deployment of American forces and the capability to project military power abroad; as mentioned earlier, these include the calls in Congress for U.S. troop reductions in West Germany and the Republic of Korea.

The Mansfield Resolution calling for the reduction of American forces in Europe fell only twelve votes short of a majority in the Senate in November 1971. During the debates on the Mansfield proposal a commentator for Radio Moscow, Tass international service, reported on May 16, 1971:

> This proposal has a powerful attraction not only for economic considerations—a reduction of military spending in Western Europe would ease the deficit of the U.S. balance of payments. The U.S. public also realizes that the preservation and building up of troops and armaments in Central Europe leads to a dangerous intensification of tensions in that area, while a reduction of troops and armaments would facilitate a normalization and improvement of the overall political climate in Europe and in the whole world.[44]

Mansfield's bill was interpreted by Soviet observers as demonstrating that "the most farseeing and sober-minded U.S. politicians are realizing that Washington's former policy—aimed at establishing

---

[43] Yu. V. Katasonov, *SShA: Voyennoye programmirovaniye* (The United States: Military Programming) (Moscow: Izdatelstvo Nauka, 1972). Excerpts in JPRS 60435, *Translations on USSR Military Affairs*, No. 975 (November 1, 1973), p. 39.
[44] Cited in *FBIS*, "Daily Report—Soviet Union," May 17, 1971, p. A-1.

U.S. hegemony in the world—has long since become outdated."[45] Accordingly, Soviet commentators assert that public support for American military deployment overseas in peacetime is rapidly diminishing. The subsequent efforts of Mansfield[46] and other senators to reduce U.S. troop strength abroad, cut appropriations for defense and limit military assistance and foreign aid are cited as evidence of this trend.

Operational Capabilities of the U.S. Military

Soviet planners assess American military capabilities by examining and integrating a broad range of factors. They recognize many aspects of the military establishment which may combine to play an important role in determining its effectiveness, both in combat and in carrying out its peacetime mission. Some of the most important elements, in Soviet eyes, that affect the operational capabilities of the U.S. armed forces include weapons systems; human factors such as morale, military discipline and combat readiness; and the military doctrine which guides the use of force for national defense and in the pursuit of objectives abroad.

Unlike most subjects, it is difficult to discern true Soviet perceptions of the operational capabilities of American military forces from the open press, for when these subjects are discussed, Russian analysts tend to describe rather than evaluate them. Qualitative comparisons of analogous U.S. and Soviet weapons systems in terms of their combat capabilities seldom if ever appear in open sources. Usually annotated with the phrase "based on materials of foreign writers," Russian articles on American weapons and deployments closely parallel accounts found in Western sources and are documented by numerous citations from Western military-technical journals and news magazines. Soviet perceptions, therefore, as distinct from mere descriptions, can only be inferred.

WEAPONS SYSTEMS

Armored vehicles remain the main offensive component of

---

45 Radio broadcast, Moscow Domestic Service, Leonid Lipovetskiy commentator, May 17, 1971; cited in *FBIS*, "Daily Report—Soviet Union," May 18, 1971, p. A-2.
46 "The Senator's Opinion," *Pravda*, July 18, 1974, p. 5.

Russia's ground forces. The advent of new antitank weapons and the increased hazards of the nuclear battlefield do not, in the Soviet view, significantly alter the effectiveness and central role of tanks in combat. Below is an excerpt of a correspondent's interview with Red Army General I. G. Pavlovskiy.

> (Question) Some people abroad are of the opinion that, in connection with the appearance of new means of armed struggle against tanks, including guided antitank missiles, and so forth, tanks are now losing their former significance. Is this so?

> (Answer) The question could be answered briefly. There is an age-old struggle between means of defense and means of attack. Each of these means has its own advantage. It is necessary only to utilize it skillfully in modern warfare. Despite the improvement and growth of the effectiveness of antitank weapons, tanks remain the main strike force and mobile force of the ground forces and a powerful means capable of performing important tasks in modern warfare. Moreover, compared with other types of combat equipment, they are the best adapted for decisive, maneuvering actions.[47]

The earlier views of P. A. Rotmistrov, Chief Marshal of Armored Troops, former commander of the armored forces, are consistent with Pavlovskiy's evaluation:

> With the appearance of nuclear weapons, the supposition began to be expressed abroad that tanks would soon leave the scene, as the cavalry had done. However, despite the appearance of new antitank weapons, these statements were not borne out. Tanks continue to play a very important role, and tank forces are the most promising arm of the ground forces.[48]

The Soviets recognize that a great deal of attention is devoted to armor by Western defense experts in that the main capitalist countries are continuing to reequip their ground forces and improve their organization to conform to the conditions of modern combat, particularly those imposed by the use of nuclear weapons:

> . . . steps are being taken to increase the striking power of divisions,

---

[47] Correspondent's interview with Soviet Army General I. G. Pavlovskiy, Commander in Chief of the Ground Forces, "The Armored Shield of the Motherland," *Pravda,* September 14, 1975.

[48] P. A. Rotmistrov, *Vremia i Tanki* (Time and Tanks) (Moscow: Voyenizdat, 1972), p. 274.

especially armored divisions, and to increase their maneuverability by equipping them with new tanks, armored personnel carriers and means of delivering nuclear weapons.[49]

Marshal Rotmistrov asserts that the overall trend of development in the American, West German and British ground forces is "toward greater independence for ground forces in conducting combat actions, strengthening their striking force and increasing mobility by including tank battalions in brigades and switching motorized infantry to tracked amored personnel carriers, which are becoming not just a means of transportation, but also combat vehicles."[50] With respect to research and development on the design of armored vehicles in NATO, Rotmistrov identifies the current requirements as increasing the caliber of tank weapons, increasing the traveling speed, increasing roadability and operating range and strengthening the armor against such effects of nuclear weapons as shock wave and penetrating radiation.[51] In addition, with respect to the interest in NATO standarization, he notes that the West German Leopard tank is "claiming the role of standard tank for the NATO armies" but that "the problem of organized massing of tanks in the NATO forces under the conditions of modern warfare still remains unsolved."[52]

Soviet military specialists have commented on the measures undertaken by the NATO command to counter the Warsaw Pact superiority in armor in a theater of operations in which tanks are expected to play a vital role:

> They have accorded a significant place to development and production of means of destroying armored targets, since they consider that combat against tanks is the most important task in combined-arms battle. With regard to this, antitank defense of troops at all stages of combat action has attained special significance. Views on methods and means of combating tanks exert a definite influence in formulation of defensive concepts; on the organizational structure of units and sub-units; on the building of defenses; and on plans for creating new models of antitank weapons.[53]

---

49 *Ibid.*, p. 256.
50 *Ibid.*, p. 224.
51 *Ibid.*, p. 226.
52 *Ibid.*
53 Colonel N. Nikitin, "The New in Tank Warfare," *Znamenosets*, No. 5 (May 1974), p. 38.

The Western military debate on the role of armored forces, colored by the high effectiveness of antitank weapons in the Middle East war of 1973, is seen by the Soviets to take these forms: (1) "the tank no longer rules the battlefield" and substantial changes must be made in the theory of tank warfare, the probable trend being the creation of divisions which integrate armor, mechanized infantry and fire-support helicopters; and (2) "the tank remains a formidable offensive weapon," and greater numbers of tanks should be deployed in NATO forces and a new battle tank developed more capable of overcoming current systems of antitank defense.[54] The general Soviet evaluation of the role of armor in the light of more effective antitank weapons is summarized by the author:

> The abundance of antitank means unquestionably does not preclude successful operation of tanks on the battlefield. A well-trained and coordinated crew can successfully combat antitank means. Cooperating closely with the infantry, artillery, helicopters and aircraft, tanks are capable of successfully accomplishing the missions assigned to them in combined-arms battle.[55]

The Kremlin sees a major innovation in antitank weapons and techniques in the use of helicopters. The experience gained in Vietnam has led, according to a Soviet writer, to the favoring of "fire-support helicopters as one of the most effective means of combating moving armored targets."[56] This appreciation of the helicopter's tank-fighting qualities is not limited to the United States, for "it should be emphasized that there is an ever-increasing tendency in the NATO countries to mount antitank guided missiles on so-called fire-support helicopters."[57] Citing the *Armed Forces Journal*, this Soviet writer comments on a recent exercise by U.S., West German and Canadian forces pitting the Huey Cobra and Kiowa helicopters against the Leopard tank and Vulcan self-propelled antiaircraft cannon. The writer notes the exchange rate between the vehicles and helicopters and concludes: "although these results were achieved in a test and not in actual combat, they are nevertheless indicative of the

---

[54] *Ibid.*, p. 34.
[55] *Ibid.*, p. 38.
[56] *Ibid.*
[57] *Ibid.*, p. 39. See also A. Pushkov, "Helicopters—Operating with Tanks and against Them," *Krasnaya Zvezda*, March 4, 1975.

high effectiveness of helicopters in combating armored targets."[58]

Soviet military analysts are aware of the evolving American tactics for employing helicopters as an antitank weapon:

> The conclusion was made on the basis of numerous experiments that helicopters are extremely vulnerable to tank machine guns at an altitude of 50-100 meters. Therefore it is recommended that much attention be devoted to ground-level flying and that greater use be made of reconnaissance helicopters. Scouting the targets, they must determine the best way that combat helicopters can attack them. As was noted in the journal *Infantry*, combat helicopters employing reconnaissance can attack enemy tanks at minimum height and maximum distance, thus remaining relatively invulnerable. In this case it is believed to be a good idea to combine fire and movement by approaching the object not in a straight line but by employing less vulnerable areas and terrain cover, and moving from one concealed position to another until the most advantageous conditions for making an attack are achieved. A helicopter can conceal itself behind a hill and then, climbing sharply, open fire, retreat and move to another firing position.[59]

The constant development of helicopter tactics employing fast low-level contour flying, the use of terrain features and camouflage, "pop-up and shoot" techniques, as well as improvements in speed, armor and firepower, have made the helicopter "a new, highly effective means of combat," with respect to which "the original speculative conclusions about its vulnerability on the battlefield have turned out to be exaggerated."[60] Soviet statements appear to indicate a view that helicopters have already proven their utility for air-mobile operations,[61] transport, reconnaissance and communications, direct fire support for troops, and more currently, for antitank defense.[62] Thus,

---

58 *Ibid.* It should be noted that articles in the Soviet military press extolling the virtues of helicopters as an antitank weapon do not necessarily reflect the perceptions of the Soviet high command on this issue. There is little evidence in the structure and practice of Soviet forces to suggest that the Soviets have embraced the attack helicopter to the extent they may perceive the U.S. Army and NATO forces to have done.

59 Colonel M. Belov, "Helicopter Attack," *Krasnaya Zvezda*, January 24, 1975.

60 Colonel M. Belov, "Combat and Helicopters," *Voyennyye Znaniya*, No. 12 (December 1974), p. 41.

61 See Colonel V. Babich, "Army Aviation of the USA," *Aviatsiya i Kosmonavtika*, No. 9 (September 1973), pp. 44-45.

62 See Belov, "Combat and Helicopters," p. 41.

Soviet military analysts perceive the helicopter as occupying an important role in the U.S. and other Western armies:

> As we have seen, the helicopter is now the most important material foundation of the "air mobilization" of the land forces belonging to the United States and the other NATO countries. It is thought that when they are used together with tanks, they will substantially increase the combat capabilities of combined-arms units under the conditions present in any type of war, including a nuclear war.[63]

As mentioned above, despite the development of nuclear weapons, Russian military experts maintain that armor has not lost its role as the primary offensive component of their ground forces. Similarly, they argue that the development of nuclear missiles has not affected the role of "barrel-type" artillery but that it "continues to be an important means of fire support for the troops in modern combat."[64] The experience gained in the Korean and Vietnam wars, along with "exercises and theoretical military research," has "completely refuted" predictions that barrel artillery would become obsolete. Consequently, the large capitalist states are said to be "devoting increasing attention to the development of conventional types of arms, primarily artillery."[65]

Soviet analysts follow intently technological improvements in U.S. weapons. They pay special attention to developments which tend to substitute weapons systems for combat personnel or enable a few soldiers to accomplish tasks formerly requiring larger numbers. Reasons for Washington's interest in automating combat methods and systems include the desire to avoid having to commit one's ground forces to action; the hope to "depersonalize" combat operations; and the need to lower the costs of war.[66]

In the Soviet view, an enemy widely dispersed and hidden from the air is largely immune to all but the most massive use of untargeted, area bombardment. Soviet authors, referring to the Viet-

---

[63] Colonel M. Belov in *Krasnaya Zvezda*, January 5, 1974.

[64] Colonel V. Nadin, Candidate of Technical Sciences, "Artillery Continues to Develop," *Voyennyye Znaniya*, No. 6 (June 1974), p. 43.

[65] *Ibid.*, p. 42.

[66] Colonel I. Grabovoy, Candidate of Military Sciences, "In Search of Super-Accurate Weapons," *Krasnaya Zvezda*, August 6, 1975.

namese experience, note that American military specialists have sought to overcome this problem with the development of precision-guided munitions—both aerial bombs and artillery shells. Soviet observers have concluded that laser-homing "smart" bombs have made it possible "to raise considerably the effectiveness of air operations in destroying bridges, storehouses, production buildings, fuel and lubricants depots, ammunition and individual tanks and motor vehicles."[67] A Soviet writer, basing his article on reports in the foreign press, notes that of 1000 bombs of this type, more than half hit their targets. This increased accuracy sharply lowers the expenditure of munitions:

> It is considered abroad that, by using guidance systems, it has in fact become possible to reduce the area on which air bombs are dropped to a magnitude equal to their kill radius. According to American specialists, expenditure on air weapons is being reduced more than one-hundredfold by this means.[68]

The improvement of guided bombs is said by Soviet commentators to make the weapons less expensive, raise bombing effectiveness under bad visibility conditions and increase bomb range by improving the weapon's aerodynamic characteristics. The use of laser-guided munitions, the Soviets observe, has now been extended to artillery shells:

> . . . According to specialists of the U.S. Army, the use of guided artillery shells which home on the target at the final stage of the trajectory makes it possible to achieve a 50 to 70 percent probability of hitting the target with the first round fired. Moreover, although the cost of firing the new type of shells can be up to fifteen times the cost of firing nonguided shells, their effectiveness is one hundred times that of the latter.[69]

Precision-guided munitions are seen by Moscow as having anti-tank applications as well. In their descriptions of this new guidance technology, they single out the helicopter-launched antitank missile Hellfire and the Lance tactical missile:

The Lance tactical missile system is being adapted for use against

---

[67] *Ibid.*
[68] *Ibid.*
[69] *Ibid.*

tanks and other combat vehicles. According to American specialists, the equipping of the missile with 9-15 terminally guided strike elements, each of which can strike an individual armored vehicle, considerably raises the combat effectiveness of this weapon system.

It is considered that the creation of cassette-type missiles with homing strike elements will make it possible to close the gap in the antitank weapons system and will ensure that enemy armored vehicles can be engaged not only in forward areas but also behind the enemy lines and in areas in which reserves and second and third echelons are deployed.[70]

In their discussion of armor, antitank weapons, helicopters and artillery, the rare evaluations made by the Soviets often appear to minimize the impact of technological advances upon the accepted role of basic ground-force weapons, such as tanks and artillery. Even with the prospect of nuclear weapons being employed extensively and in depth throughout a theater of operations, the utility of tanks and artillery has not been reduced, in Soviet opinion, and may in some cases have been enhanced. This is because armor offers protection from blast, infrared and penetrating radiation and permits the rapid exploitation of contaminated areas. Furthermore, the development of nuclear munitions for conventional artillery expands the role of these weapons. The advent of precision-guided munitions, launched by air, from artillery or by means of surface-to-surface missiles, permits accurate, deep and effective strikes against enemy forces. The Russians appear to think, in fact, that precision-guided munitions may be more useful in many combat situations than tactical nuclear weapons. Whether or not this will lead to a revision of Soviet views on the use of tanks, infantry, artillery and the organization of rear services remains to be seen.

Many Soviet discussions concerning the U.S. Air Force stress two major themes: the effects of the Vietnam War and the development of new aircraft. Soviet treatments of those topics are usually quite factual, simply citing the views of Western sources and offering little or no hint of the actual Soviet perception. Occasionally, however, Soviet analysts do evaluate American strategy or doctrine:

... in the process of the development of the art of war ... extreme opinions have sometimes appeared resulting from a one-sided or

---

[70] *Ibid.*

simply incorrect evaluation of the results of one or another combat event or of the actual effectiveness of means of attack. As examples of such extreme opinions one might cite repeated assertions after World War II by some U.S. Air Force leaders about the possibility of conducting independent air war. . . . Gen. Arnold of the U.S. Air Force . . . recommended that long-range bombers be used to suppress centers of potential military danger in Europe and in Asia. Somewhat different, yet still quite close overall to Arnold's views, were the reflections on this subject by U.S. Air Force Gens. Spaatz and Doolittle. Variations in those views were apparently reflected in the methods of military operations in Korea and Vietnam.[71]

More detailed analyses of the U.S. Air Force examine the impact of combat experience in Vietnam on American electronic warfare capabilities, ground attack techniques and responses to antiaircraft defenses. Improvements in American capabilities are described in some detail and examples of the North Vietnamese response are cited when appropriate. The following examples are indicative of such studies:

> . . . air strikes in North Vietnam began with aircraft not prepared to offer electronic countermeasures to antiaircraft systems. . . . It was extremely difficult to develop tactical procedures directed at reducing the effectiveness of new antiaircraft resources. . . .
>
> The information received with the aid of radio technical reconnaissance was used for warning crews of strike aircraft of the launching of enemy antiaircraft missiles. . . . However, the look radar lacked apparatus for selection of low-flying aerial targets against the surface. This deficiency was skillfully exploited by North Vietnamese fliers carrying out sudden and fruitful attacks from below on the aerial enemy.[72]

Such analyses consistently suggest that the Kremlin takes very seriously the capabilities of the U.S. Air Force. On the other hand, Soviet writers assert that Russian air-defense technology gave the North Vietnamese an excellent record of success in destroying American planes.

---

71 Professor Rear Admiral N. Pavlovich, "Basic Factors in the Development of the Art of Naval Warfare," *Voyenno-Istoricheskiy Zhurnal*, No. 12 (December 1974), p. 52.
72 Colonel V. Babich, "The Tactics of 'Radio-electronic Warfare,'" *Aviatsiya i Kosmonavtika*, No. 4 (April 1975), pp. 46-47.

Soviet writers similarly follow with great interest the development, testing and deployment of new U.S. aircraft. Soviet evaluations, as distinct from descriptions, of such aircraft are terse or nonexistent; the analysts usually prefer to quote Western opinions. For example, in describing the F-15, one Soviet officer commented dryly, "If the advertising reports are to be believed, the F-15 will be the most maneuverable and fastest fighter in the world."[73] The same analyst made the observation that "the 'North American' company ... asserts that the B-1 has the most natural design of any military aircraft."[74] At most, Soviet sources will summarize the planned capabilities of a given aircraft without discussing its probable effectiveness against Russian forces. To illustrate, after summarizing the ability of the B-1 to penetrate air defenses by low flight and electronic countermeasures, the Soviet analyst remarked:

> . . . all this is done in order that the aggressor aircraft can overcome the enemy air-defense system and carry its death-dealing cargo deep into enemy territory. This cargo is an extremely substantial one: 22 tons of bombs, and in the overload variant up to 45 tons.[75]

When reporting deficiencies or problems encountered by U.S. aircraft—as in the F-111A or the C-5A—Soviet analysts continue to cite only Western opinions:

> The F-111A . . . is reported to be the most highly perfected night and all-weather aircraft. But it has also been revealed that the F-111A has not met its tactical-technical requirements. For example, its range has turned out to be 4426 kilometers instead of the planned 6727 kilometers; its speed exceeds the speed of sound by only 2.2 times instead of the planned 2.5 times; and its takeoff weight is 37,410 kilograms rather than the planned 31,335.[76]

---

73 Engineer Colonel N. Kon'kov, "Speed, Altitude and Maneuverability," *Bloknot Agitatora*, No. 18 (September 1973).

74 Engineer Colonel N. Kon'kov, "A New Weapon of Aggression," *Bloknot Agitatatora*, No. 17 (September 1974).

75 *Ibid.*, p. 16.

76 Kon'kov, "Speed, Altitude and Maneuverability," p. 13. For fuller discussions of U.S. Air Force tactics and Soviet antiaircraft defenses, see Colonel V. Babich, "The Tactics of Evasion," *Aviatsiya i Kosmonavtika*, Nos. 9 and 10 (September and October 1974); B. T. Surikov, *Raketnyye sredstva boy'by s nizkoletyashchimi tselyami* (Rocket Means of Combat with Low-Flying Targets) (Moscow: Voyenizdat, 1973); S. A. Peresada, *Zenitnyye raketnyye kompleksy* (Surface-to-Air Missile Systems) (Moscow, 1973).

Soviet writings on the U.S. Air Force are so reserved in their content that it is extremely difficult to deduce the underlying perceptions. From the very topics of their articles and the consistent themes, however, it is clear that Soviet analysts regard the technological sophistication of modern U.S. aircraft as a major strength. The fact that American aircraft, personnel and doctrine have all been tested in combat reinforces this perception, although it is perceived to be offset to some extent by the rather considerable combat testing which Soviet air-defense equipment received in Vietnam.

Since the creation of submarine-launched ballistic missiles, naval forces have grown in significance from their already important role as one of the chief means to project military power and political influence abroad. As Fleet Admiral of the Soviet Union Sergey G. Gorshkov puts it:

> The constantly growing capabilities of navies to carry out strategic missions is elevating their role in warfare. The significance of the oceanic theaters of military operations is also being elevated accordingly. As a result, an even further increase in the scale of naval warware as one of the most important parts of warfare as a whole is foreordained.[77]

Because of the strategic role of navies, enhanced by the growing capabilities of strategic missile-carrying submarines to carry out missions against land targets from ever-greater distances, as well as the corresponding growth in the dimensions of antisubmarine operations and systems designed to counter other naval strategic nuclear weapons platforms, "naval combat activity may embrace almost the entire expanse of the world ocean and take on a global character."[78] In the light of this Kremlin view, it is not surprising that many Soviet discussions of the U.S. Navy focus on its global-strategic role and the means by which it is fulfilled:

> It is well known that despite the favorable changes in the world the militarist forces in the United States and certain other countries are not abandoning their imperialist course. . . . In their attempts to pursue a policy of global supremacy, they allocate a big role to the Navy. . . . In order to accord with this ocean strategy, surface ships

---

[77] Admiral S. G. Gorshkov, "Certain Questions Concerning the Development of the Naval Art," *Morskoy Sbornik*, No. 12 (December 1974), p. 24.
[78] *Ibid.*

should have high mobility, great independent range and greater combat stability.[79]

Because nuclear propulsion grants surface and submarine vessels virtually unlimited range, nuclear-powered ships are seen by the Soviets as one of the chief means by which the U.S. Navy will maintain its global role.[80] It is noted, for example, how nuclear power has dramatically increased the capabilities of aircraft carriers:

> . . . the range at full speed of the U.S. aircraft carrier *Enterprise*, as the press reports, is 140,000 miles, and at 20 knots, it is 400,000 miles, whereas the range of conventional aircraft carriers does not exceed 8000 miles—during combat action in Vietnam, the nuclear aircraft carrier *Enterprise*, accompanied by other nuclear-powered ships, stayed on station in the combat region for up to 50 days without returning to base. Conventional aircraft carriers, however, would have had to return to base to replenish stocks after 15-30 days. Moreover, the great speed of a nuclear aircraft carrier, in the opinion of the U.S. Naval Command, ensures it better protection against submarine attacks and makes it difficult to carry out air strikes against it.[81]

Reflected in this detailed description of the *Enterprise* is the respect the Soviets appear to have for all aspects of advanced American naval technology, including automated fire-control and target-identification systems, communications, electronic countermeasures, as well as specific weapons systems such as ASW platforms and their missiles, mines and torpedoes,[82] and SLBMs.[83] A repeated theme in Soviet military writings is that superior technology may exercise a potentially decisive impact on the outcome of naval engagements,

[79] Reserve Captain 1st Rank A. Zheludev, Professor and Candidate of Naval Sciences, "Nuclear-Powered Surface Ships," *Krasnaya Zvezda,* January 16, 1974.

[80] *Ibid.*

[81] *Ibid.* It should be noted, however, that this writer overemphasizes the importance of nuclear propulsion power in enabling a carrier to stay on station. Even nuclear carriers require replenishment of aviation fuel, ammunition, food and general stores, provided by underway logistic ships. Conventionally powered carriers fueled and supplied at sea can remain on station approximately as long as nuclear-powered carriers. Presumably, Soviet naval planners are generally better informed on this question than the writer quoted here.

[82] See A. A. Kvinitskiy, *Protivolodochnoye oruzhiye i yego nositeli* (Antisubmarine Weaponry and Its Carriers) (Moscow: Izdatelstvo DOSAAF, 1973).

[83] See Naval Captain G. Svyatov, head of a sector in the Institute for the Study of the United States and Canada, USSR Academy of Sciences, "Missiles from the Depths," *Voyennyye Znaniye,* No. 2, (February 1974), pp. 40-41.

implying the need for the USSR to compete aggressively with the United States in the development of advanced weapons:

> Along with the use of surprise based on secrecy and the speed of operations of the attacking and supporting force, it is impossible to ignore the possibility of technical surprise . . . the use of technical surprise only yields the appropriate result when these new means are used in sufficient quantities for attainment of the goal.[84]

One of the areas of great technological sophistication which has provoked significant Soviet comment concerns SLBMs, in particular the MIRVed Trident missile. Admiral Gorshkov notes that "the naval ballistic missile being developed in the USA, it is believed, will have a range of more than 10,000 km and, in principle, harbors great capabilities for trajectory maneuver to hit targets within vast areas."[85] The fascination Soviet authors manifest in considering the prospects of technological innovation occasionally leads them to treat seriously Western projections even of a more speculative nature. Illustrative of this, Admiral Gorshkov notes:

> The American press is already writing of the possible development of a fundamentally new type of aircraft carrier which will be equipped with powerful engines and will be in the form of an air-cushion surface ship developing speeds up to 190 knots (333 km/hr), i.e., some 5 times greater than present carriers.[86]

In their overall evaluation of American naval capabilities, Soviet commentators pay the highest possible compliment to the U.S. Navy: they integrate American strategic experience into their own doctrine and planning. For example, in their views on the relationship between operations and amphibious assaults, Russian naval strategists stress the lesson of American combat experience:

> The moment will come in combat operations when it is necessary to consolidate the successes achieved, to occupy and hold a certain space, which will require a landing on the enemy's territory by large troop groups. Combat operations in Korea and Vietnam confirm that submarines and aviation can meet the requirements of

---

84 Professor Rear Admiral N. Pavlovich, "Basic Factors in the Development of the Art of Naval Warfare," *Voyenno-Istoricheskiy Zhurnal* (Military-Historical Journal), No. 12 (December 1974), p. 50.
85 Gorshkov, *op. cit.*
86 *Ibid.*

landing such a quantity of troops to a lesser degree than surface vessels.[87]

The sources summarized above indicate that Soviet observers perceive several major strengths in the U.S. Navy: great range and endurance; heavy firepower; increasingly modern weapons systems; and strategic and tactical doctrine which has been tested in combat. Consistent with their view of American forces in general, the Soviets stress the political role of the U.S. Navy and view it as a major component in the maintenance of America's global power.

HUMAN FACTORS

According to Soviet spokesmen, a correct evaluation of the strength of armed forces must take into account not only weaponry but also human factors. As Minister of Defense and Marshal of the Soviet Union A. A. Grechko has stated:

> While attaching great significance to the technical equipment of the Armed Forces, the Party has always considered that armaments and technical equipment are not, in themselves, the decisive factor. The main thing is the people in whose hands the means of struggle are found.[88]

In this sense, political awareness and ideological conviction are regarded as "the basis for all of the success of Soviet fighting men."[89] For example, the conference report of the All-Army Conference of Experts in Combat and Political Training held in May 1975 declared:

> Only an ideologically convinced, disciplined, and intelligent soldier or sailor, possessing high combat moral qualities and strong physical conditioning, can master and employ with maximum effect the weapons entrusted to him to achieve victory over the very strongest enemy.[90]

---

[87] *Ibid.*

[88] Marshal of the Soviet Union A. A. Grechko, "The Leading Role of the CPSU in the Construction of the Army of a Developed Socialist Society," *Voprosy Istorii KPSS*, No. 5 (May 1974), p. 42.

[89] "Multiply the Ranks of Expert Trainees," *Kommunist Vooruzhennykh Sil*, No. 13 (June 1975), p. 11.

[90] *Krasnaya Zvezda,* May 30, 1975.

Similar importance is attached to the psychological qualities of soldiers:

> A soldier, deeply loyal to his homeland, but not possessing these special psychological qualities, can lose his head in battle, yield to panic, and not fulfill the combat mission. Based on their own combat experience, participants of the war know how it was difficult originally to adapt to a combat situation and to overcome the psychological barrier of a sense of danger. An "experienced" soldier acts confidently in battle not because he is indifferent to danger, but rather because he was taught "to subordinate passion to reason." This circumstance evoked a special trend in the education of troops —psychological training.[91]

Consequently, psychological training is considered to be "the foundation of all other qualities essential to a guardain of the Fatherland."[92] As one Soviet source has noted:

> The morale of the army plays a decisive role in the war because, as a material force, it can raise or lower the fighting efficiency of the troops. Only if morale is high can all the hardships of the modern armed struggle be endured and military equipment be used with the greatest efficiency. Low morale damages the fighting qualities of the troops. . . . *A high morale cements the other elements of the combat power of the troops, multiplies their strength.*[93]

Based upon this outlook, Russian spokesmen demonstrate considerable interest in the sociopolitical foundations of America's armed forces. In the Soviet view, armies are class-based organizations which reflect the strengths and weaknesses inherent in their respective social systems. It follows from this view that the socialist system, possessing an inherently superior sociopolitical foundation, will have the greater potential for perfecting its human factor. Conversely, since the capitalist system is by nature exploitative and contradictory, the armies of capitalist states can be expected to experience many serious problems. The Vietnam War is credited with having magnified these problems.

---

91 Colonel N. Tabunov, "V. I. Lenin—The Founder of the Theory of Communist Education," *Kommunist Vooruzhennykh Sil,* No. 2 (January 1974), p. 16.
92 "Methodological Recommendations," *Kommunist Vooruzhennykh Sil*, No. 7 (April 1974), p. 24.
93 *Marxism-Leninism on War and the Army*, p. 352. Emphasis in the original.

Moscow's general argument is that the Vietnam War lowered the combat capability of U.S. forces by exacerbating racial tensions, creating a serious drug problem and generally eroding respect for the leadership and authority of officers. According to one Soviet officer, racial conflicts are "the number one problem of the U.S. armed forces."[94] Drug usage also receives considerable attention:

> According to the American press, by the end of the Vietnam War in several sub-units of the U.S. Army up to 90 percent of the assigned personnel were regularly using drugs. The number of drug addicts in the American Army reached many hundreds of thousands. Things went so far as to include the discovery of drug addicts aboard one of the American atomic submarines on duty and armed with ballistic missiles.[95]

Such factors have led to a lack of respect for authority. Just as the proletariat is supposed to be in revolt against the bourgeoisie in capitalist society, so the common soldier is described as naturally being in opposition to the officer stratum.[96] It is noted, for example:

> Under conditions of an existence without purpose, surveillance [of their personal activities] and denunciations, American soldiers and sailors are developing feelings of deep hostility toward everything taking place and hostility toward their commanders and their uniform. American servicemen are trying to distract themselves from the ugly reality that surrounds them, to forget themselves with the help of alcohol and drugs. This in turn provides for the further loss of spirit and the spreading of a feeling of indifference and inconsolability.[97]

In the Russian view, American NCOs are assigned the role of the "basic executive unit" and are "directly responsible for training and indoctrinating the personnel."[98] The war in Vietnam revealed that "a considerable part of the American noncommissioned officers were

---

94 Captain 3rd Rank G. Grachikov, "What They Teach Them," *Krasnaya Zvezda*, June 17, 1975.
95 N. Seregin, "Drug Addicts in American Uniforms," *Sovetskiy Patriot*, February 23, 1975.
96 Captain 1st Rank T. Belashchenko, "Ideological Indoctrination in the Armies of NATO Countries," *Voyennyy Vestnik*, No. 5 (May 1972), pp. 114-15.
97 N. Seregin, "The U.S. Army: Corrosion of the Spirit," *Sovetskiy Patriot*, February 12, 1975.
98 Grachikov, *op. cit.*

incapable of providing 'moral leadership' and effectively directing their subordinates in combat."[99] Moreover, American NCOs are singled out as being the particular target of the soldier's hostility:

> . . . there were frequent cases of open hostility between the non-commissioned officers and the lower ranks in the U.S. expeditionary force in Vietnam. American psychiatrist Robert Lifton, who studied the problem of interrelations between soldiers and non-commissioned officers, acknowledged that the "war between the lower ranks and the noncommissioned officers was sometimes fiercer than that between the American Army and the Viet Cong." . . . In their conversations with Lifton, many soldiers frequently declared that they "often felt the urge to turn their weapons against their true enemies—the sergeants."[100]

Given the heavy emphasis placed on discipline within the Red Army, these factors have probably engendered some question as to the reliability and effectiveness of American soldiers. The problems in the U.S. military of decaying morale, lack of military discipline, drug abuse and racial strife receive prominent attention in the Soviet press. While undoubtedly this emphasis to some extent is intended to serve a propaganda purpose, it likely affects to some degree the Soviet perceptions of U.S. forces and modifies Soviet assessments of American military capabilities.

In the peacetime disposition of forces these problems are readily observable. Not only are U.S. servicemen unruly and unkempt:

> American soldiers lazily loiter around the area of their base. The majority of them have their hands in their pockets and their collars are carelessly unbuttoned. No one pays any attention to the orders and commands of his superiors. On the steps leading into the barracks they play cards, smoke, and use foul language . . .[101]

But they are also susceptible to antimilitary propaganda:

> Speaking of the attitudes of groups of servicemen in the U.S. Army, one cannot fail to note the growth of antiwar protest arising from the extremely unpopular American aggression in Vietnam. Furthermore, there are underground antimilitary organizations publishing antiwar newspapers for soldiers. Some of these assuredly are simply

---

99 *Ibid.*
100 *Ibid.*
101 Seregin, *op. cit.*

pacifist, but a few have a sharp political orientation that produces considerable uneasiness in the command. To an undetermined extent this naturally results in a weakening of the morale and combat effectiveness of the imperialist armies.[102]

Perhaps reflecting their recognition that conditions may change in a combat situation, Soviet observers are adamant in asserting that these factors have not rendered the capitalist armies impotent. While these trends have adversely affected U.S. combat potential, the capitalist armies continue to be a serious threat. Noting that "it would be wrong to overestimate the influence of such factors," the above-cited author pointed out that the Soviet Union must retain its vigilance:

> Imperialist armies and first of all the U.S. Army are a dangerous weapon for aggression and piracy in the hands of war provocators. These armies are large, armed with modern weapons, well prepared and well trained.
> The comprehensive training of these armies for war, the uses to which they are put in suppressing the workers of their countries and the national liberation forces of other countries, demands vigilance from the Soviet people and the peoples of all fraternal states.[103]

It is necessary to exercise some caution in drawing conclusions about the Soviet assessment of human factors affecting American military capabilities, especially when these conclusions are based on the open Soviet press. Negative descriptions of the morale and discipline of U.S. troops have obvious propaganda value for both domestic and foreign consumers. It would also be unwise, however, lightly to dismiss these public articulations, for in some cases the accounts are factual, and may reflect actual perceptions. But Soviet military planners appear not to perceive them as exercising a decisive influence on the overall fitness, readiness and combat capability of America's armed forces.

U.S. STRATEGY AND MILITARY DOCTRINE

Military doctrine is a broader concept in Soviet usage than is the case in the United States. Doctrine is seen as "depending directly on

---

[102] Belashchenko, *op. cit.*, p. 115.
[103] *Ibid.*

the social structure, the state problems with regard to domestic and foreign policy, and the economic, political and cultural state of the country."[104] Furthermore, Soviet spokesmen illustrate their analyses of the changes in the U.S.-Soviet power relationship by tracing and asessing the evolution of U.S. strategic and foreign policy doctrines over time.[105] Marshal V. D. Sokolovskiy offers a broad definition of doctrine:

> Military doctrine is the expression of the accepted views of a state regarding the problems of political evaluation of future war, the state attitude toward war, a determination of the nature of future war, preparation of the country for war in the economic and moral sense, and regarding the problems of organization and preparation of the armed forces, as well as the methods of waging war. Consequently, by military doctrine one should understand the system of officially approved, scientifically based, views on the basic fundamental problems of war.[106]

In the publicly expressed Soviet view, the initial manifestation of Washington's attempts to adapt to the changing correlation of forces brought about by the emerging military strength of the USSR was the abandonment of the doctrine of massive retaliation and its replacement in the early 1960s by the "flexible response" strategy. Although viewed as a partial retreat, "flexible response" was regarded as a further attempt by American military planners to broaden the applicability of military force "by strengthening those of its components which would make it possible—while abstaining from a nuclear war against the USSR—to conduct with impunity so-called local wars."[107] The American failure in Vietnam, in the Soviet view, marked the demise of flexible response as a viable strategy, since it demonstrated the inability of the United States to convert military power into political objectives under the conditions where

---

104 Harriet F. Scott, translation of Marshal of the Soviet Union V. D. Sokolovskiy, *Military Strategy* (3rd ed.; New York: Crane, Russak & Company, 1974), p. 38.

105 See G. A. Trofimenko, "Military-Strategic Aspects of the 'Nixon Doctrine,'" in Yu. P. Daviydov, V. V. Zhurkin and V. S. Rudnev, eds., *Doktrina Niksona* (Moscow: "Nauka," 1972), pp. 54-80; G. A. Arbatov, "The Stalemate of the Politics of Force," *Problemy Mira i Sotsializma* (Problems of Peace and Socialism), No. 2 (February 1974), pp. 41-47; M. A. Mil'shteyn and L. S. Semeyko, "The Problem of the Inadmissibility of a Nuclear Conflict (On New Approaches in the USA)," *SShA*, No. 11 (November 1974), pp. 2-13.

106 Scott, *op. cit.*

107 G. A. Arbatov, "Soviet-American Relations at a New Stage," *Pravda*, July 22, 1973.

the correlation of world forces had changed in favor of the Soviet Union. Washington was then impelled to change its policy of intervention and instead adopt a strategy of "local wars by proxy" and "burden sharing" with its allies and clients. These enforced changes were embodied in the Nixon Doctrine.

With the Nixon Doctrine came two related policies. First, there was an attempt by the U.S. leadership to seek more friendly relations with the Soviet Union—this took the form of "détente." Second, there was an effort to stabilize military relations between the superpowers through the SALT negotiations and agreements. The Soviets allege that the most recent U.S. initiative in the field of military doctrine, the limited strategic (or selective counterforce) options policy, is a means of compensating for U.S. weakness.[108]

Soviet military writers have long rejected the concept of limited nuclear war. In the late sixties, following the debates on U.S. counterforce strategy and tactical nuclear war, Marshal V. D. Sokolovskiy wrote in his *Military Strategy* on the dangers of escalation inherent in limited nuclear war:

> Various limitations are mostly forced and conditional. A limited war is fought with a tremendous danger of escalating into general war, especially if tactical nuclear weapons are used. This is also recognized by American theoreticians.[109]

Thus, in various respects, the negative Soviet reaction to the "Schlesinger Doctrine" is similar to their response to various past doctrinal attempts to rationalize strategic theory, such as the flexible response and city avoidance counterforce concepts. Soviet military writers observed in 1969:

> To lull the vigilance of the peoples, the U.S. militarists are discussing the possibility of limiting the nuclear war. . . . The deliberate falsehood of these assurances is easily exposed. The propaganda of "limited wars" is intended to pacify public opinion, to accustom people to the thought that nuclear war is possible. At the same time, all talk about confining nuclear strikes only to military objectives is intended to camouflage the plans for a preemptive war (first strike) against the socialist countries.[110]

---

[108] Mil'shteyn and Semeyko, *op. cit.*, p. 11.
[109] Scott, *op cit.*, p. 69.
[110] *Marxism-Leninism on War and the Army*, p. 100.

The public Soviet position on limited or controlled nuclear war has changed little in this respect. Current published Soviet views on flexible and selective strategic options reject the concept of controlled nuclear warfare. Commenting in July 1974 on the "imperialist circles' formula of 'controlled' limited nuclear war," with its "regulation of the methods of war and the fixing of rules for waging it," Colonel V. V. Larionov referred to the prospect of escalatory nuclear holocaust and noted that, "perfectly understandably, the Soviet Union resolutely opposed this approach to the problem."[111] Shortly thereafter, two Soviet specialists on U.S. military doctrine wrote in the journal of the Institute for the study of United States and Canada (IUSAC):

> Many Pentagon strategists essentially do not wish to change their military-political principles and are continuing to seek ways and opportunities to use nuclear weapons. . . . However, the possibility of unleasing a "small" and "painless" nuclear missile skirmish and keeping it within safe limits is a myth which in no way corresponds to the realities of nuclear war.[112]

Soviet references to the "Schlesinger Doctrine" have included a suggestion that the "qualitative improvements of arms" necessary to operationalize such a strategy would ensure for the United States military-technical supremacy over the socialist countries. The limited nuclear options (LNO) proposals have also been described as a psychological device—a political rather than a military strategy:

> . . . all the talk of Pentagon officials about "retargeting" such missiles does not at all represent some sort of objective information on changes in the proposed tactics of the military use of American strategic forces, being published for the information of the general public, but is a deliberate attempt to exert psychological pressure upon the other side, an attempt to derive if not direct military-technical gain then, at least, a conceptual, psychological advantage in relation to the other side.[113]

On the basis of the arguments presented above, it seems evident

---

111 Colonel V. V. Larionov, "The Relaxation of Tension and the Principle of Equal Security," *Krasnaya Zvezda*, July 18, 1974.
112 Mil'shteyn and Semeyko, *op. cit.*, pp. 9-10.
113 G. A. Trofimenko, "Problems of Peace and Security in Soviet-American Relations," *SShA*, No. 9 (September 1974), p. 17.

that the Soviets regard LNO as a destabilizing factor in the strategic balance between the U.S. and USSR. The Soviets are clearly concerned that the United States might implement an LNO strategy; and they portray it as an aggressive initiative with preemptive or first-strike implications. In addition, they claim that it is detrimental to the pursuit of peaceful coexistence and further strategic arms agreements between the superpowers.[114]

Paradoxes and Ambivalences

In no area is it more difficult to sort out the meanings and implications of Soviet images of the United States and the worldwide superpower competition than in Moscow's views of American military power. A major reason for this lies in the fundamental paradox that it is precisely the possession of overwhelming Soviet military strength that has permitted the nonmilitary aspects of the global systemic competition to be enhanced in importance. As observed in earlier chapters, the correlation of forces is an aggregate of many factors—including the military—which determine whether the socialist states are prevailing in the struggle with world capitalism. Now that the Soviet Union has achieved strategic nuclear parity, so the argument goes, the USSR can exploit with impunity worldwide, ideological, political, economic, social and scientific-technological trends which will bring about socialist victory. The capitalists, of course, seeing that they are losing the ongoing struggle—termed "peaceful coexistence"—would like to revert to military solutions. The growing might of the Soviet armed forces, however, forecloses such options. Thus the paradox: as peaceful coexistence comes to be the accepted norm of superpower competition, so it becomes ever more necessary to increase the strength of Soviet military forces.

---

114 For a discussion of how limited nuclear options provides "Pentagon militarists" a "trump card" at SALT and creates a new arms race in the qualitative rather than quantitative sphere, see *ibid.*, p. 17; M. G. Vladimirov, "The Arms Agency Report," *SShA*, No. 7 (July 1974); Mil'shteyn and Semeyko, *op. cit.*, p. 11: ". . . the creation of highly accurate nuclear attack facilities, that is, their continuous qualitative improvement . . . is nothing other than the arms race in its most complex and, perhaps, most dangerous—the *qualitative*—sphere." Emphasis in the original.

It may be, of course, that this concept, which has given Soviet foreign policy such a military cast, really means that "in the sphere of Soviet security interests and defense policy . . . ideology . . . has given way to a 'pseudo-ideology' all its own."[115] However true, it gives to Soviet views of the American military an importance that would not otherwise be the case. And perhaps more importantly, the Soviet government has acted in accordance with this concept, clearly rejecting the idea of parity or rough equivalence in military strength with the United States in favor of a policy of pursuing superiority. This surprised many American national security leaders; this development, however, is consistent both with Soviet definitions of peaceful coexistence and with the importance assigned to military power in assessing the correlation of forces.

Such a Soviet view also leads to ambivalent estimates of American military power. On the one hand, the Kremlin's military leaders want to make certain that their armed forces can cope with those of NATO and the United States. Like their counterparts everywhere, they tend, therefore, to see the opposing military as very formidable, threatening and dangerous. Such perceptions ensure that national security continues to receive a disproportionate share of Russian resources, at the expense of other sectors of the economy. At the same time, it is ideologically necessary to insist that NATO is fraught with internal dissension and gradually growing weaker. The United States, in particular, is seen as waning in strength, although still militarily formidable. Soviet military leaders solve this basic dilemma essentially by distinguishing between the human elements of American (and Western) military power and the weapons system components. Individual American soldiers are seen as much more poorly indoctrinated, motivated and disciplined than their Soviet counterparts. Authority throughout American society is claimed to be breaking down; this especially affects adversely the armed forces, with ordinary soldiers no longer willing to accept direction from their officers. Furthermore, the lack of esteem by the general public for the military has seriously degraded the fighting capability of U.S. armed forces.

In contrast to their low opinion of American military personnel,

---

115 John Erickson, "Détente: Soviet Policy and Purpose," *Strategic Review*, Spring

the Soviets appear to have high regard for U.S. weapons systems. They seem especially impressed with the technological sophistication of American weaponry and follow developments in U.S. weapons systems assiduously. No doubt this also makes it easier for Soviet military leaders to persuade—if they need persuading—civilian elements in the ruling hierarchy to continue to accord high priority to Russian weapons research, development and procurement.

With regard to particular U.S. military services, it seems likely that the Soviets admire the American Navy most highly. This may stem from the fact that the Soviet Navy is quite inexperienced in warfare as compared to that of the United States. In any event, Soviet admiration can be clearly inferred from Soviet emulation of American naval strategy and operational techniques. Naval technology is repeatedly stressed as potentially decisive in the outcome of naval conflict, indicating that the Soviets will continue to stress research and development in such areas as antisubmarine warfare and precision guidance of sea-based missiles. In a strategic sense, it is certain that the goal of the Soviet Navy is to be able to operate globally, as does the United States, in order that Soviet objectives of extending their power and influence worldwide, after a long era of "imperialist encirclement," may be at last achieved.

Whether Soviet attitudes about American military might—a mixture of contempt and admiration, fear and confidence—represent their true beliefs or not, it is almost surely the case that their expressed views lead the outsider to conclude that Moscow will continue to place the highest priority on further developing its already formidable military machine. Definite military superiority, not parity with the United States, is the goal of the Soviet leadership.

The 25th Congress of the CPSU and Beyond

THE PARTY CONGRESS, according to CPSU statutes, is "the supreme organ of the Communist Party of the Soviet Union."[1] Yet, since 1927, the institution has served as a rubber stamp for decisions previously made by the Party's leadership, and indeed from that time forward all decisions and resolutions have been passed unanimously by the Congresses. There are many reasons for the evolution in the nature of the Party Congresses of the CPSU, of both a practical and a political character. From a practical standpoint, the Party Congress, with its some five thousand delegates[2] and brief, one-week sessions, is ill suited for the discussion, debate and formulation of national policy. Political constraints, too, have undermined the role originally intended for the Congresses. Intra-Party policy debate to raise and clarify issues prior to the convening of the Congress was prohibited

---

[1] "Statutes of the Communist Party of the Soviet Union," *XXII s"yezd Kommunisticheskoy partii Sovetskogo Soyuza. Stenograficheskiy otchet* (22nd Congress of the Communist Party of the Soviet Union), Vol. III (Moscow: Politizdat, 1962), p. 346.

[2] For example, during the last three Party Congresses, the number of delegates has been: 4943 (1966); 4963 (1971); and 4998 (1976). See the speeches of I. V. Kapitonov, chairman of the Mandate Commission, at the respective congresses, in *XXIII s"yezd Kommunisticheskoy partii Sovetskogo Soyuza. Stenograficheskiy otchet* (23rd Congress of the Communist Party of the Soviet Union. Stenographic Record), Vol. I (Moscow: Politizdat, 1966), p. 279; *XXIV s"yezd Kommunisticheskoy partii Sovetskogo Soyuza. Stenograficheskiy otchet* (24th Congress of the Communist Party of the Soviet Union. Stenographic Record), Vol. I (Moscow: Politizdat, 1971), p. 331; and *Pravda*, February 28, 1976.

by a resolution at the Tenth Congress of the CPSU (1921).[3] Designed to halt ongoing factionalist debates then splitting the Party, the resolution was an outcome of Lenin's efforts to enforce greater discipline and unity within the Party. Thus the trend which culminated in the present domination of Party Congresses by the highest executive organs of the CPSU (the Politburo, the CPSU Secretarist and the Central Committee) began early with Lenin and was later fully realized under Stalin's rule. As originally conceived, delegates to the Congress were to be elected from among the local Party membership; in actuality, the selection of delegates was made by the Party executive. Consequently, the CPSU Party Congress rapidly declined as the institution holding supreme authority in the determination of Party policy to that of a pro forma gathering in which the delegates endorse decisions made previous to the Congress and "elect" those of the CPSU hierarchy whose ascendancy to the highest-ranking posts has been prearranged by the executive organs of the CPSU.

In view of its current primary role as a rostrum for publicizing past "achievements" and charting future policy directions, the Party Congress offers an important opportunity for Western observers to witness the Party elite introduce, explain and justify the domestic and foreign policy of the USSR to both internal and external audiences. Additionally, at certain times in Soviet history, most notably the immediate post-Stalin period and the Khrushchev era, the Party Congresses have been the forum for significant changes in Soviet policy—changes of vital importance for the Soviet system itself, its allies and its adversaries. At the 20th Congress in 1956, for example, Nikita Khrushchev delivered his famous "Secret Speech" concerning the "cult of the individual," denouncing Stalin for his crimes and beginning the period of de-Stalinization for Soviet society. This Congress was also marked by important foreign policy statements. In his Accountability Report, Khrushchev advanced the proposition that war between socialism and imperialism was no longer fatalistically inevitable, thus further laying the foundations for the contemporary Soviet strategy of peaceful coexistence. Noting that the world situation had "changed radically" insofar as the "world camp

---

3 "On the Unity of the Party," *Desyatyy s"yezd RKP(b). Stenograficheskiy otchet* (Tenth Congress of the RKP(b). Stenographic Record) (Moscow: Politizdat, 1963), p. 571.

of socialism" had become a "mighty force" with the moral and material means to prevent aggression, Khrushchev observed:

> War is not fatalistically inevitable. Today there are mighty social and political forces possessing formidable means to prevent the imperialists from unleasing war, and if they actually try to start it, to give a smashing rebuff to the aggressors and frustrate their adventurist plans.[4]

Among other important changes ushered in by the 20th Congress was the further revision of Stalin's rigid "two camp" theory, which defined the world as divided into the unalterably opposed camps of socialism and capitalism. Under the new world conditions, Khrushchev identified changes such that there was an emergence "in the world arena of a group of peace-loving European and Asian states which have proclaimed non-participation in blocs as a principle of their foreign policy," a "vast peace zone" which "embraces tremendous expanses of the globe, inhabited by nearly 1.5 billion people—that is, the majority of the population of our planet."[5] Asserting that the forces of imperialism were growing weaker as the "centuries-old mainstays of colonialism are crumbling and the peoples themselves are, with increasing boldness, beginning to decide their own destinies," Khrushchev observed with reference to this Third World that:

> For the creation of an independent national economy and the raising of the living standard of their peoples, these countries, although they do not belong to the world socialist system, can draw on its attainments. Now it is not necessary for them to go cap in hand to their former oppressors for modern equipment. They can receive such equipment in the countries of socialism without paying for it with obligations of a military or political nature.[6]

In general, during the Khrushchev era, the competition between the two systems was envisioned as a struggle by means short of general war through which the Soviets would attain victory because of

---

[4] N. S. Khrushchev, "Accountability Report of the Central Committee of the Communist Party of the Soviet Union to the 20th Party Congress," in *XX s"yezd Kommunisticheskoy partii Sovetskogo Soyuza. Stenograficheskiy otchet* (20th Congress of the Communist Party of the Soviet Union), Vol. I (Moscow: Politizdat, 1956), pp. 37-38.

[5] *Ibid.*, pp. 22, 24.

[6] *Ibid.*, p. 25.

the inherent superiority of the socialist system. According to Khrushchev, the "advantages" of the socialist economic system would gradually receive increasing recognition.[7] In time, this would lead to a preponderance of forces favorable to socialism, an alignment from which even more favorable conditions would be developed. Thus, Khrushchev asserted in a report to the 21st Party Congress in 1959 on the new seven-year plan that:

> Fulfillment of the plan will increase the economic potential of the USSR to such an extent that, coupled with the growth of the economic potential of all socialist countries, it will secure a decisive preponderance in the correlation of forces in the international arena in favor of peace, and thus will come into existence new and still more favorable conditions for averting world war and preserving peace on earth.[8]

As these references indicate, Khrushchev took the opportunity presented by the occasion of Party Congresses to announce significant changes in Soviet foreign policy. Major innovations and redirections in Soviet policy toward the West were promulgated. Firmly established in this regard were theses related both to avoidance of war between the USSR and the United States and to economic competition between the two systems which further clarified the meaning of "peaceful coexistence." Reiterated also was support for national liberation movements and the need to continue to develop Soviet military power.

The 25th Party Congress: Continuity in Soviet Policy

In the hands of Khrushchev's successors, Congresses have been more deliberate, prudent and notable for their emphasis on continu-

---

[7] For example, in an interview given to I. McDonald, foreign editor of *The Times* (London) on January 31, 1958, Khrushchev remarked: "The time is not far off when we shall overtake the most advanced capitalist states and outstrip them in per capita output. Everything now points to this, and when it has been achieved the indisputable superiority of the socialist system will be even more obvious to everyone." See N. S. Khrushchev, *For Victory in Peaceful Competition with Capitalism* (New York: E. P. Dutton & Co., 1970), p. 91.

[8] N. S. Khrushchev, "On the Planned Figures for the Development of the USSR National Economy in 1959-1965," *Vneocherednoy XXI s"yezd Kommunisticheskoy partii Sovetskogo Soyuza. Stenograficheskiy otchet* (Extraordinary 21st Congress of the Communist Party of the Soviet Union. Stenographic Report) (Moscow: Politizdat, 1959), p. 72.

ity in policy. The recent Congress revealed no major departures from policies elaborated at the 23rd and 24th Party Congresses. Indeed, the innovation, the daring and bold schemes characteristic of the late 1950s and early 1960s, have seemed inimical to the leadership since Khrushchev's ouster in October 1964.

The 25th Congress appeared to reflect the style of the current regime. In the broadest sense, the tone created by the Soviet delegates (in contrast to a few non-Soviet visitors) was calm, confident and, to a degree, optimistic. The dominant themes emphasized the wisdom of the existing policy of recognizing and applauding "successes" alleged to be outcomes of past decisions. The most significant event at the Congress was the conflict between the CPSU and Communist parties of Western Europe, which flared into unexpected intensity. However, the overall businesslike atmosphere of the recent Congress proceedings does not render it any less important for the analysis of Soviet foreign policy. Rather, it is precisely the continuity, optimism and confidence displayed in the speeches by Brezhnev and other Soviet delegates which provides an important indicator of the nature and long-term direction of Soviet foreign policy. It reflects their underlying belief in the correctness of the current strategy for victory in the struggle with the West, a strategy in large measure formulated upon the Soviet perception of the West and its foremost power, the United States.

In contrast to past CPSU Congresses, the only person to deliver a major speech on foreign policy was Brezhnev.[9] In the Accountability Report, approximately one-third of the text was given over to foreign affairs. The fact that the General Secretary alone among the Party hierarchy delivered a major address on this topic again emphasized not only Brezhnev's further consolidation of his preeminent

---

9 The events of the 25th Congress indicate that Brezhnev's political vitality remains undiminished. In the proceedings themselves, Brezhnev clearly stood out as the dominant figure. His vigorous 5-hour, 15-minute report, and his energetic behavior, interrupting speakers with questions, comments and asides, belie the speculation about his declining health. Another indicator of Brezhnev's power and authority is exorbitant and extravagant praise heaped upon him prior to and during the 25th Congress by Soviet and foreign delegates. The remarks of V. I. Prokhorov, head of the trade unions, were not atypical. He referred to Brezhnev as "an eminent figure of the Leninist type," with "enormous experience, worldly wisdom, fast-growing and astonishingly accurate philosophical observations and generalizations and the knowledge of everything that constitutes the substance of the laboring person's life." *Pravda*, March 4, 1976.

position in the Politburo, but also the united front presented by the Party on issues related to foreign policy. In contrast to Party tradition, the speeches of both the Minister of Defense (Grechko) and the Minister of Foreign Affairs (Gromyko)—both of whose speeches would conceivably have dealt at length with foreign affairs—were struck entirely. Moreover, the contributions of Chairman of the Council of Ministers Kosygin on foreign economic matters have significantly declined over the past three Congresses; this trend continued to the extent that there was virtually no foreign policy content in his speech to the 25th Party Congress. For these reasons, an analysis of the foreign policy aspects of the recent Congress must focus the bulk of its attention on Brezhnev's Accountability Report.

The fundamental bases of Soviet policy toward the West have changed little since 1964. The hallmark of this policy has been the present regime's consistent emphasis on peaceful coexistence as the basic principle in East-West state relations. For example, in the new regime's first major foreign policy statement following the sudden ouster of Khrushchev, Brezhnev reassured the uncertain West by saying that "the Soviet Union has been and is pursuing the Leninist policy of peaceful coexistence of states with different social systems."[10] Then, at the 23rd Party Congress (1966), Brezhnev asserted that "while exposing the aggressive policy of imperialism, we are at the same time consistently and unalterably pursuing a course toward peaceful coexistence of states with different social systems."[11] Similarly at the 24th Party Congress (1971), he reiterated this point, noting that the Soviet "principled line with respect to capitalist countries, including the USA, is consistently and fully to implement the principles of peaceful coexistence . . ."[12] This common theme was reaffirmed by the General Secretary in the Accountability Report to the 25th Party Congress:

> The main factor in our policy with respect to the capitalist states has been and remains the struggle for the affirmation of the prin-

---

[10] *Pravda*, November 7, 1964.

[11] L. I. Brezhnev, "Accountability Report of the Central Committee of the CPSU to the 23rd Congress of the Communist Party of the Soviet Union," in *XXIII s"yezd*, I, 43-44.

[12] L. I. Brezhnev, "Accountability Report of the Central Committee of the CPSU to the 24th Congress of the Communist Party of the Soviet Union," in *XXIV s"yezd*, I, 51-52.

ciples of peaceful coexistence, for lasting peace, for the lessening, and in the long run, the elimination of the danger of the outbreak of a new world war.[13]

Spanning the decade of the Brezhnev era, these references illustrate the continuing vitality of this Soviet precept. It should be noted that not only has this formula survived, but it has lasted virtually unchanged, despite many waverings in Soviet-American relations and the attainment of strategic military parity by the USSR. Indeed, the theme of peaceful coexistence has, in fact, been expressed in almost every significant Soviet foreign policy statement since 1964, no matter what the source or circumstance.

The element of continuity relative to Soviet statements on peaceful coexistence since 1964 is that it is conceived of and utilized as an instrument of class struggle with the West. Emphatically, it is not envisioned as a neutral policy in support of the status quo or accommodation with capitalism. At the 23rd Party Congress, for example, Brezhnev stressed that peaceful coexistence is "a form of class struggle between socialism and capitalism."[14] At the 25th Party Congress, détente, the most recent stage in peaceful coexistence, was likewise described as a means of conflict:

> Détente does not in the slightest measure abolish, and cannot abolish or alter, the laws of class struggle. . . . We make no secret of the fact that we see in détente the way to create more favorable conditions for peaceful socialist and communist construction.[15]

Brezhnev also reiterated the view at the recent Party Congress that the West has acquiesced in the principles of peaceful coexistence, not because Western leaders in general are desirous of friendly relations, but because the shift in the correlation of international forces in socialism's favor has forced them to confront "reality" and yield to Soviet demands for peace. "The transformation from 'cold war'

---

[13] *Pravda*, February 25, 1976. Subsequent references to Brezhnev's 25th Party Congress speech, unless otherwise noted, are found in this source.

[14] Brezhnev, "Accountability Report . . . to the 23rd Congress," p. 44.

[15] This view of détente and its utility for the class struggle was corroborated in the remarks of foreign delegates. For example, in his address, the chairman of the National Council of the Communist Party of India observed: "Détente not only is not inhibiting the struggle of anti-imperialist and democratic forces, but, on the contrary, is promoting the struggle and unification of these forces and constantly widening this unity." *Pravda*, February 29, 1976.

and an extremely dangerous confrontation of the two worlds to a relaxation of tensions," said Brezhnev, "was connected primarily with the changes in the correlation of forces in the world arena."

Applying this general proposition to the Third World, the General Secretary argued that "with the present correlation of world class forces, the liberated countries are fully able to resist the imperialist diktat and to achieve just—that is, equitable—economic relations." Furthermore, in addition to the general shift in the correlation of world forces, Brezhnev noted that the liberation of these nations from "imperialist" exploitation was facilitated by the active support of the Soviet Union. However, he carefully distinguished Soviet support for national liberation movements and anti-Western regimes from Western assistance, which Moscow characterizes as being given solely in the selfish interest of the capitalist state donor. According to the General Secretary:

> The Soviet Union does not interfere in the international affairs of other countries and peoples. An immutable principle of the Leninist foreign policy is respect of the sacred right of every people and every country to choose its own path of development. However, we make no secret of our views. In the developing countries, as everywhere, we are on the side of the forces of progress, democracy and national independence, and regard them as our friends and comrades in the struggle.
>
> Our party renders and will render support to peoples who are fighting for their freedom. In so doing the Soviet Union is not searching for advantages for itself, is not hunting for concessions, is not striving for political domination and is not seeking military bases.

Moreover, Brezhnev responded to Western critics of Soviet foreign policy who argued that support for national liberation is in conflict with the principles of peaceful coexistence and détente. He maintained that such arguments indicated "either naïveté or, more likely, a deliberate clouding of the mind." In this respect, Brezhnev reminded his audience, both at the Congress and abroad, that peaceful coexistence and détente apply only to interstate relations with the West. Since the Soviets define national liberation movements as a "class" phenomenon, they are said to transcend the realm of normal state-to-state relations. Conversely U.S. activity in the Third World is depicted as totally evil and is censured in the most vilifying terms.

nists in various countries who are making "a compromise on matters of principle or a reconciliation with views and actions opposing Communist ideology," demeaning proletarian internationalism, or who go so far as to reject internationalism outright. Particularly subject to Soviet criticism were those Western European Communist parties resorting to "opportunism" (namely, those parties which pursue the parliamentary path to power, accept the alternation of parties and reject the principle of dictatorship of the proletariat). Brezhnev reaffirmed that proletarian internationalism—which since the time of Lenin and the failure of world revolution has meant in Communist parlance the obligatory subservience of foreign CPs to Moscow's direction—remains "the sacred duty of every Marxist-Leninist." In even more strident fashion, P. M. Masherov, First Secretary of the Belorussian Communist Party Central Committee, chastised those CPs following a policy independent of proletarian internationalism:

> Unfortunately there are still champions of socialism, who, under the pretext of the defense of their so-called "originality" and national peculiarities, are essentially revising the principles of proletarian internationalism and emasculating the revolutionary essence of Marxism-Leninism and its class-action nature. Moreover, every aspostasy from revolutionary teaching is represented as an innovation, but the actively living movement of Marxist-Leninist theory and its embodiment in the practice of socialism are qualified as conservatism and dogmatism. As is well known, however, history puts everything in its place. The objective laws of social development and class struggle cannot be ignored.[19]

While support for this position by some foreign Communist parties was forthcoming,[20] notable exceptions were made by the British, French, Italian and Yugoslavian delegates, all of whom stressed the role of "national peculiarities" in the "struggle for socialism." Indeed, it has been argued by some Western analysts that one reason for the failure of Georges Marchais, First Secretary of the French

---

[19] *Pravda*, February 26, 1976.

[20] See, for example, the speech by Todor Zhivkov, in which the First Secretary of the Bulgarian Communist Party Central Committee maintained that "attitude toward the Soviet Union is the touchstone of revolutionary character, and the watershed between the forces of progress and the forces of reaction." *Pravda*, February 27, 1976.

Communist Party, to attend the 25th CPSU Congress was his desire to demonstrate publicly French independence in the face of Soviet attempts to impose its definition of proletarian internationalism on Western European communism.

In retrospect, the 25th Party Congress appears to support the earlier thesis that Soviet foreign policy has shown marked continuity under the Brezhnev regime. This is particularly the case with regard to Soviet relations with the Western world in the post-Vietnam War era. The events at the Party Congress suggest, therefore, that Soviet leaders have found little in the years since the 24th Party Congress to substantially alter their views of the capitalist world. To the contrary, their reaffirmation of past policy at the recent Congress would appear to indicate that their images of the West in general and the United States in particular have in fact been reinforced. Given Soviet confidence in the correctness of their appraisals and thus the unlikelihood of major changes, one can with some assurance project at least the major outlines of Soviet policy toward the United States in the next few years.

Détente and the Future of Soviet-American Relations

Given Russian power today, there can hardly be a more critical task for political analysis than asking: What do the Soviets intend to do with their vast might? What are likely to be the broad outlines of future Soviet policy toward the United States? Forecasting future Soviet conduct is a hazardous enterprise, of course, as those who have attempted it will testify. Nevertheless, the images Soviet leaders have of America and its role in world affairs should yield at least a few clues about the future. Unfortunately, the propositions which form the core of Soviet analyses of American society and government reflect unfavorably on the United States. Especially damaging to viable Soviet-American peaceful coexistence is the firm Soviet conviction that it was a change in the correlation of forces that compelled the United States to adopt the policy of détente. Thus Soviet leaders do not perceive the attempts of the American government to negotiate issues, to ameliorate the arms race, to encourage trade and so on as indicating any genuine desire for peace. On the contrary, these are involuntary acts forced on a still hostile and aggressive

America. Accordingly, indications that the United States really would like to improve superpower relations do not induce reciprocal feelings on the part of Soviet leaders.

The Russians also see the United States as weakened and divided by severe internal strife. Part of this image is derived from the Marxist intellectual framework, which sees class conflict as endemic in capitalist society. Beyond this, however, are the views Moscow has from firsthand observation of tensions between the New Left and the establishment, between blacks and whites, young and old, and even between the legislative and executive branches of government. The Soviets appear to think that the recession of the early 1970s, the oil embargo and the Watergate affair have exacerbated the tensions and magnified the hostilities between groups of Americans, even extending to the "ruling groups" and the "military-industrial complex," weakening their faith in their ability to govern the United States.

Soviet perceptions of the United States can be inferred from Soviet policy behavior, of course, as well as from content analysis of Soviet statements. Here, too, the evidence is very disquieting. Especially significant is the fact that the ink on the June 1973 détente agreements—intended above all else to prevent superpower confrontation and conflict—was scarcely dry when the most serious Soviet-American clash since the Cuban missile crisis of 1962 occurred in the Middle East during the fourth Arab-Israeli war in October 1973. In this confrontation, the Kremlin dispatched messages to the White House which were described as "brutal" and of the character of ultimatums and readied airborne divisions for direct military intervention in the Middle East. Goaded by Soviet threats, attacked by congressional critics and pressured by Israel, the U.S. administration finally responded with a worldwide alert of American strategic forces, thus directly threatening the Soviet Union. These actions by the superpowers made a mockery of the idea of détente.

More significant than the "political signals" exchanged between the USSR and the United States during the crisis, however, was the fact that the Soviet Union was attempting to alter the balance of power in an area of the world of enormous strategic and economic significance to the West. Moscow's leaders knew full well that Soviet domination of the Middle East, with its strategic location and vital oil resources, would pose literally a life-or-death threat to America's

Western European and Japanese allies and thus imperil the entire structure of East-West relations. Less critical but nonetheless significant, orchestrated Soviet-Arab oil actions would seriously damage the American economy and substantially increase worldwide inflationary pressures. Nevertheless, just prior to, during and immediately after the Yom Kippur War the Soviet government took a number of highly provocative actions:

- Arming to an unprecedented degree Egypt, Syria and Iraq, all of which were in confrontation with countries allied to or friendly with the United States. After 1967 the Soviet government did not provide the Arabs with the quantity and quality of weapons necessary for renewed conflict with Israel. Beginning in the spring of 1973, however, Soviet-Egyptian relations improved and understandings apparently were reached on new Soviet arms deliveries. Thus an attack on Israel became a reasonable policy option. Without the qualitative and quantitative increase in weapons deliveries in the spring and summer of 1973 and Soviet pledges of diplomatic support, there would have been no Yom Kippur War.

- Urging the Arabs to use the oil weapon. For some years the Soviet government had argued that the Arabs should embargo oil to the Western nations unless they ceased supporting Israel. Moscow at various times also argued that the Arabs should manipulate their currency holdings in such a way as to damage Western financial institutions. The Soviets have long urged oil-producing states to raise significantly the price of their oil. Finally, the Soviet government for many years has attempted to persuade the oil countries to nationalize the oil companies and to take oil properties without compensation, thus helping to "liquidate imperialism" in the Middle East.

- Failing to inform and consult with the United States, as required by the Nixon-Brezhnev agreements of May 1972 and June 1973,[21] in order to attempt to prevent the impending Arab attack on Israel

---

21 In the "Basic Principles of Relations Between the USA and the USSR," signed in Moscow on May 29, 1972, the two powers agreed "to do everything in their power so that conflicts or situations will not arise which would serve to increase international tensions." *Weekly Compilation of Presidential Documents*, VIII No. 23 (June 5, 1972), 943. In the "Agreement on Prevention of Nuclear War," signed in Washington on June 22, 1973, the United States and the USSR agreed that anytime there appeared to be a risk of nuclear conflict the two countries "shall immediately enter into urgent consultations with each other and make every effort to avert this risk." *Department of State Bulletin*, July 23, 1976, pp. 160-61.

with its attendant risk of escalating to an American-Soviet confrontation.

- Failing to support U.S. initiatives for a cease-fire in the Security Council of the UN on October 8, 1973, and appealing to other Arab states, such as Algeria and Morocco, to join in the conflict. The Soviet government supported U.S. efforts to halt the conflict only after Israeli military successes and only in order to prevent an Arab military disaster.

- Resupplying of the Arabs during and after the war, including the provision of SCUDs and advanced MIG fighters. Since the War Syrian armed forces have been especially strengthened. Soviet arms agreements also have been signed with the Libyan government, probably the most violently anti-Western regime among the Arab countries.

- Threatening direct Soviet armed intervention during the war.

- Supporting maximum Arab demands on Israel, just short of the extinction of the Israeli state.

These actions by the Soviet government were in direct contravention of Soviet-American agreements of 1972 and 1973 and could in no way be called consistent with the spirit of détente proclaimed as governing superpower relations. Yet the United States government did not hold the Soviet leaders even verbally accountable for their flagrantly aggressive behavior in the Middle East. In fact, Washington, although obviously displeased with Moscow, clearly preferred to downplay the extent to which détente had proved illusory; to acknowledge this is to admit a failure in national security policy not as dramatic as the collapse of America's Southeast Asia posture but in the long run much more threatening.

Contributing also to Russian confidence that the correlation of forces is shifting in favor of the Soviet Union was the total collapse of cooperation among the industrial powers during the oil embargo of late 1973 and early 1974, bringing into sharp focus serious problems in transatlantic relationships. It has been estimated that the Arab oil embargo had by January 1974 involved a reduction of less than 10 percent in their pre-embargo (September 1973) shipments to the oil-importing countries.[22] Nevertheless, the initial Arab decisions to

---

22 William Schneider, *Food, Foreign Policy, and Raw Materials Cartels* (New York: Crane, Russak & Company, 1976), p. 4. Schneider's computations are based on data from the *Petroleum Intelligence Weekly*.

reduce production and impose the selective embargo against the United States and the Netherlands led to a number of actions by oil consumers designed to appease the Arabs and avoid further reductions in their oil supplies:

- The countries of Western Europe by and large refused to cooperate with the United States and instead competed to see which country would prove itself most pro-Arab. This non-cooperation was most immediately evident in their refusal (with the exception of Portugal) to permit the United States to overfly their territories or to use their ports in resupplying Israel. (The West Germans did permit covert use of Bremerhaven, but after this became public knowledge, they notified the United States that they would not permit further usage.)

- Fellow members of the EEC felt themselves unable to come to Holland's aid by sharing their oil for fear of being embargoed themselves.

- Japan resisted the intense pressure from the Arab oil producers to sever relations with Israel, but it did become decidedly pro-Arab in its diplomatic stance.

- Black African nations (twenty-one in all) broke relations with Israel in order to curry favor with the oil-rich Arabs.

- In November 1973, Saudi Arabia forced Aramco to cut off products derived from Saudi oil to U.S. military forces. This created a potentially dangerous situation for the Sixth Fleet.

- Saudi pressure was also applied to the Philippines, resulting in a government order that no Philippine-processed oil or oil products would be sold to the U.S. military after November 15. Singapore also ordered oil companies to halt sales to the U.S. military.

These maneuvers demonstrated the inability and the unwillingness of the consuming states to take effective counteraction against the oil producers. Even a hint of collaboration with the United States was scrupulously avoided by the more vulnerable nations. In view of near-panic behavior on the part of Western European leaders,[23] is it surprising that Soviet spokesmen viewed these events as

---

[23] For a slashing attack on European reactions to the Arab oil embargo, see Walter Laqueur, "The Idea of Europe Runs Out of Gas," The New York Times Magazine, January 20, 1974.

confirming their convictions concerning deep and irreconcilable contradictions within the capitalist world, and especially between the United States, Western Europe and Japan? Indeed, this Soviet image of the state of Western weakness in the face of adversity is apparently shared by many Americans as well.

Undoubtedly, the Soviet view of Western disunity has encouraged Moscow to believe that its long-sought goal of expelling the American presence from Western Europe is attainable. The centerpiece of Soviet national security concerns is the alleged threat from NATO. Accordingly, the neutralization of Europe remains a prime objective of Soviet foreign policy. While NATO is certainly not as strong militarily as the Warsaw Pact, it nevertheless still represents the strongest aggregation of military force opposing the Soviet Union. Furthermore, the productive resources of the Western European economies, their sophisticated technological base and pool of skilled manpower, the incomparably higher standard of living enjoyed in Western Europe and the resilient web of sociopolitical traditions and institutions pose a significant challenge to Soviet-dominated Eastern Europe. As long as this condition exists, Moscow will feel its empire threatened. Thus any sign of division between Western Europe and the United States—whether it is the disarray which accompanied the Arab oil embargo, a move in the United States to reduce its military presence in NATO or the alleged remarks of American officials condoning Soviet domination in Eastern Europe—is eagerly greeted by Moscow. Soviet policy toward Europe is to maintain a divided Germany within a divided and disunited Europe which will gradually disengage itself from the United States. Whether the appropriate term for this policy is the "Finlandization of Europe" is questionable; there is no doubt, however, as to the substantive content of Soviet goals. And certainly transatlantic relations since 1973, the "successful" conclusion of the 1975 Helsinki Conference on Security and Cooperation in which the "legitimacy" of Soviet domination of Eastern European countries was "recognized" by President Ford, and the general euphoria of détente, have encouraged Soviet leaders to continue to hope for the neutralization of Western Europe within the foreseeable future.

Moscow's détente policy plays an important role in this endeavor, for it makes it appear, to both the Western Europeans and the Americans, that the threat from the Soviet Union has receded. NATO, accordingly, will be seen as no longer vital. It is probable, also, that the tolerance now shown by the Kremlin for independent courses of action by Western European Communist parties stems at least in part from the desire not to alarm NATO governments. This is not to say that Soviet leaders are pleased with the defiance shown them by Western European Communists. It is to suggest, however, that this is not the great setback for Moscow seen by some observers. On the contrary, even if the Soviet government is concerned, it nevertheless fits well with détente strategy.

Just as the Soviet leaders see the possibility of weakening transatlantic ties, so they believe that the future will lead to a widening breach in America's relations with its principal ally in Asia, Japan. Characterizing the Japanese-American relationship as undergoing a "crisis of confidence," Soviet leaders claim that the USSR offers Japan an alternative to their reliance on the United States. At the same time, Soviet policy toward Japan is becoming increasingly tough—to the point of arrogance—as Soviet military power grows and American strength in Asia continues to recede. Basically, Soviet leaders are ambivalent toward Japan. On the one hand, they desire, as in the case of Western Europe, to persuade Tokyo that its future lies in being "neutral" in the Soviet-American worldwide struggle. On the other hand, confidence born of a perceived shift in the correlation of forces leads to an uncompromising stance on issues dividing Japan and the USSR, not conducive to detaching Japan from its alliance with the United States. To date Soviet overtures to Japan have been limited to offering investment "opportunities" in Siberian oil and gas development, making efforts to increase the already substantial volume of Soviet-Japanese trade and suggesting that Japan support Soviet proposals for an Asian "collective security" arrangement.

Of far greater importance to the Soviet Union's posture in Asia is its confrontation with China. Soviet perceptions concerning the People's Republic of China have been consistently negative for some time. The emergence of China as a great power with enormous political, economic and military potential has heightened its diplomatic influence among developed, established nation-states as well as its ability to compete for influence and limit Soviet gains in the Third World. The rapprochement between the United States and the People's Republic of China, and China's admission to the United

Nations, have exacerbated the problem the Soviets refer to as the "Chinese factor." Soviet strategy to cope with the "Chinese factor" is characterized by both conflict and competition. The competition is carried out primarily in the Third World and among revolutionary movements, while conflict and confrontation are manifest in both the interstate and the international diplomatic arenas. Soviet spokesman have charged that China is seeking hegemony in Asia, contrasting this with Soviet efforts to establish an Asian collective security system to "benefit" the Asian people. This scheme and other Soviet policies indicate the apprehension with which Moscow views possible Chinese dominance in Asia. In assuming the role of pre-eminent patron of North Vietnam in the later stages of the war, and assisting India's successful effort during the 1971 Indian-Pakistani war to bring about the dismemberment of Pakistan, a major Chinese ally, the Soviet Union has sought to offset or limit the expansion of Chinese influence in the Asian subcontinent.

The Soviet leadership is obviously apprehensive about the possibility of a Sino-American rapprochement directed against the USSR. Undoubtedly, this fear played a motivating role in Soviet détente policy and acts as a partial restraint on Soviet behavior which would lead the United States to reject détente. Moscow seems especially concerned about a possible Sino-Japanese-American coalition directed at the Soviet Union. This perception seems more relevant to Soviet policy in Asia than the oft-mentioned rivalry between the two Communist countries in the Third World.

Soviet views of the role of the less developed countries in world politics have evolved through several phases. Under Stalin's regime Soviet attitudes toward the Third World countries reflected a lack of understanding of the situation in which nationalist and Communist movements found themselves in the period following World War II. Preoccupied with the Communization of Eastern Europe, the problem of Germany and Russian relations in the Greek-Turkish-Iranian area, Soviet leaders paid only cursory attention to most of the developing world. Consistent with the so-called Zhdanov Doctrine, revolutionary leaders in the still dependent areas, such as Nehru of India, Sukarno of Indonesia and U Nu of Burma, were dismissed as imperialist lackeys. And when these countries achieved their independence, Soviet leaders viewed it as a "cunning fiction," concealing the reality of their continued reliance on their former colonial masters.[24] All countries remained part of the British and American camp until they became part of the Soviet empire. This two-camp logic was the basis of the Stalinist theory and practice of cold war.[25]

While there were hints of a return to the pre-1928 "rightist" approach at the 19th Communist Party Congress in Moscow in 1952, it was not until Khrushchev emerged as the dominant figure in the Soviet collective leadership that a more realistic policy toward the Third World was adopted. Finally recognizing the strategic implications of a Third World hostile to the West, the Soviet government began to compete vigorously with the United States through providing economic aid, military aid and technical assistance to selected Third World countries.[26]

The Soviets soon learned that the problems of the Third World in many cases were intractable. Furthermore, Soviet leaders discovered that economic and military aid did not automatically result in Soviet influence over recipient governments, win permanent friends for the Soviet Union or even ameliorate their harsh treatment of local Communists. Nevertheless, by and large Khrushchev remained hopeful about Moscow's chances of expelling the West from the Middle East, Asia and Africa, thus altering irrevocably the world balance of power in favor of the Soviet Union.

Khrushchev's successors viewed developments in the Third World with much less optimism. By late 1965, while still repeating traditional slogans of Soviet support for the worldwide liberation struggle, the Kremlin apparently had decided to downgrade its efforts in the Third World.[27] Furthermore, Soviet analyses of Third World countries became increasingly pessimistic about the early transition of these nations to socialism. Instead, the main consideration as to whether a developing country was accorded special treatment by Moscow was its foreign policy orientation, not its internal economic, social or even political character.[28]

---

[24] Robert C. Tucker, *The Soviet Political Mind* (New York: Praeger, 1963), p. 191.
[25] *Ibid.*
[26] For a survey of Soviet economic aid to less developed countries, see Marshall I. Goldman, *Soviet Foreign Aid* (New York: Praeger, 1967). For an analysis of Soviet military aid programs, see Wynfred Joshua and Stephen P. Gibert, *Arms for the Third World* (Baltimore: The Johns Hopkins University Press, 1969).
[27] Morton Schwartz, "The USSR and Leftist Regimes," *Survey*, Spring 1973, p. 218.
[28] Stephen P. Gibert, "Wars of Liberation and Soviet Military Aid Policy," *Orbis*, Fall 1966, pp. 852, 858.

Subsequent to the Arab-Israeli war of October 1973, Soviet views of the Third World once more became more optimistic. There appear to be several reasons for this. First, Moscow, with its great emphasis on the foreign policy postures of the less developed countries, tends to see trends as favorable or unfavorable depending upon whether events damage or weaken the West in general and the United States in particular. The weak and divided reaction of the NATO countries to the Yom Kippur War and the subsequent oil embargo certainly reinforced the Soviet perception that the Third World can be an important arena of struggle between East and West. Second, the failure of the United States government to attack Soviet adventurism in the Middle East as a violation of détente was viewed as another bit of evidence that the correlation of forces had shifted in Moscow's favor. Soviet and American leaders alike recognize that the oil embargo touched off a new wave of anti-Western feeling in the poorer countries; everywhere demands are being heard for a "new economic order."

Soviet spokesmen apparently see the United States, still in post-Vietnam War shock, as being unwilling to resist Soviet-supported efforts to topple conservative regimes in the Third World. After all, the United States had proved unwilling to hold Moscow accountable for its large-scale reequipping of North Vietnamese and Viet Cong forces shortly after the 1973 truce agreements. And in 1975, when all pretense was dropped that the conflict was a civil war within South Vietnam between Saigon and Viet Cong forces, and the North Vietnamese took over the South, Moscow received no protests from Washington. That the United States would accept such a defeat for American policy in Asia, and yet continue to act as if a meaningful détente existed, could not but be interpreted in the Kremlin as anything other than the final abandonment of the historic containment policy.

For all these reasons, Soviet views of the Third World at present are more sanguine than they have been since the Khrushchev era. These favorable assessments appear to have been confirmed by the inability of the United States to counter Soviet and Cuban support for the Moscow-oriented faction in the Angolan war. Sub-Saharan Africa, unlike the Middle East, has not been accorded priority in Soviet global strategy. When an opportunity was presented, however, détente proved not to be a restraint. At the time of its independence, unlike the other Portuguese colonies (Guinea-Bissau and Mozambique), Angola found itself with no single national liberation front or movement to receive the transfer of power from Lisbon. A struggle began between the Soviet-sponsored Popular Movement for the Liberation of Angola (MPLA) and two other liberation movements, the National Front for the Liberation of Angola (FNLA) and the National Union for the Total Independence of Angola (UNITA). Soviet support for the MPLA included a massive military assistance program and sophisticated weapons, numerous Soviet and Eastern European advisers and some thousands of Cuban troops. This use of Cuban troops may be an early indication of a Soviet inclination to employ proxy war in the future—the use of surrogate armed forces from other socialist states. This has set a dangerous precedent; it seems likely that, flushed with their Angolan success, Soviet policy in the Third World has entered a new and more militant phase. Especially significant is that in intervening in Angola the Soviet government was involved in an undertaking remote from the borders of the USSR and in an area where Russia historically has not had interests.

Finally, since the very essence of détente has been stated repeatedly by both Soviet and American spokesmen to be the elimination of nuclear war between the two superpowers, the ultimate test of the policy lies in the preservation of a strategic balance conducive to the maintenance of peace. The indications that the Soviets, in pursuing their military buildup, are not intending merely parity but are attempting to acquire meaningful military superiority over the United States is the single most ominous development since détente began. Among knowledgeable persons, particularly those who practice the arcane arts of comparative force posture analysis, there is a widespread consensus concerning the formidable and growing Soviet military power. To repeat, the question now is not, as it was during the Khrushchev era, whether the Soviets will achieve strategic parity, but whether they will be able to gain clear military superiority over the United States and to what uses Moscow will put such supremacy if (or when) it is achieved. In that connection, most American observers of Soviet-American relations in the past (including the present author) have described Soviet conduct in world affairs as expansionist but nevertheless prudent and cautious. Additionally, some analysts have tended to dismiss Soviet ideology as meaningless; a more or less stable discrepancy has been noted between Soviet rhetoric and foreign policy behavior. It may be the case, however, that the "stable discrepancy" has not been between rhetoric and behavior but between Soviet intentions and capabilities. The world has had no experience with a Soviet Union that has achieved parity and beyond with the United States. Past studies of Soviet risk-taking behavior, accordingly, are not likely to be reliable guides to Moscow's future conduct.

An analysis of Soviet images of the United States and the ongoing competitive struggle between the two superpowers cannot but lead one to a pessimistic view of the future. A more antagonistic Soviet-American relationship—whether called "cold war" or some other name—would appear to be nearly inevitable. When this will occur will depend upon how quickly Americans understand the vast gulf that separates the illusion of détente from the reality of a confident and expansionist Soviet Union, determined to become the dominant world power.

A Note on Russian Sources

THE MAJORITY of data employed in this study was gleaned from the all-union newspapers and specialized journals published in the Soviet Union. With the exception of such journals as *International Affairs*, *Soviet Military Review*, and *New Times*, which are published in several languages, the periodical literature examined here was in the Russian language. The use of such newspapers and journals permitted a survey of a wide range of topics and spokesmen. The following soviet periodicals were selected for their authoritativeness and particular relevancy to this study of Soviet images of the United States:

Aviatsiya i kosmonavtika (Aviation and Aeronautics), monthly journal of the USSR Ministry of Defense.

Bloknot agitatora (Agitator's Notebook), semimonthly journal of the Main Political Administration (MPA) of the Soviet Army and Navy.

Ekonomicheskaya gazeta (Economic Gazette), weekly economic newspaper of the CPSU Central Comittee (CC CPSU).

International Affairs, English-language monthly journal of the All-Union "Znaniye" Society.

Izvestiya (News), daily of the USSR Council of Ministers.

Kommunist (Communist), major theoretical and political journal of the CC CPSU, published 18 times per year.

Kommunist Vooruzhennykh Sil, *(Communist of the Armed Forces)*, semimonthly journal of the MPA.

Krasnaya Zvezda (Red Star), daily of the Soviet Ministry of Defense.

Mirovaya ekonomika i mezhdunarodnyye otnosheniya (World Economics and International Relations), monthly journal of the Institute of World Economics and International Relations, USSR Academy of Sciences.

Morskoy sbornik (Naval Digest), monthly journal of the Soviet Navy.

Novoye vremya (New Times), weekly journal of the Soviet Trade Unions, published also in English.

Pravda (Truth), authoritative daily of the CC CPSU.

Problemy Dal'nego Vostoka (Problems of the Far East), quarterly journal of the Institute of the Far East, USSR Academy of Sciences.

Problemy mira i sotsializma (Problems of Peace and Socialism), monthly theoretical journal of the Communist and Workers' parties.

S.Sh.A.: ekonomika, politika, ideologiya (U.S.A.: Economics, Politics, Ideology), monthly journal of the Institute of the USA and Canada, USSR Academy of Sciences.

Sotsialisticheskaya industriya (Socialist Industry), daily of the CC CPSU.

Sovetskiy patriot (Soviet Patriot), semiweekly of the Volunteer Society for Cooperation with the Armed Forces (DOSAAF).

Soviet Military Review, English-language monthly of the USSR Ministry of Defense.

Tekhnika i vooruzheniye (Equipment and Armaments), monthly journal of the USSR Ministry of Defense.

Vestnik Akademii nauk SSSR (Herald of the USSR Academy of Sciences), monthly journal of the USSR Academy of Sciences.

Voyenno-istoricheskiy zhurnal (Military-Historical Journal), Monthly journal of the USSR Ministry of Defense.

Voyennyye znaniya (Military Knowledge), monthly journal of DOSAAF.

Znamenosets (Standard Bearer), a monthly journal of the USSR Ministry of Defense.

The data collected from the Soviet periodicals listed above was supplemented by an examination of particularly germane monographs published in the USSR. Those monographs which offered a more comprehensive treatment of important topics than the periodical literature were specifically consulted. Soviet books and monographs cited in the text include:

G. A. Arbatov, *The War of Ideas in Contemporary International Relations*, Moscow, Progress Publishers, 1973.

V. A. Baranyuk and V. I. Vorob'ev, *Avtomatizirovannyye sistemy upravleniya shtabov i voyennykh uchrezhdeniy (Automated Control Systems for Staffs and Military Installations)*, Moscow, Voyenizdat, 1974.

V. Bolshakov, *Anticommunism, the Main Line of Zionism*, Moscow, Progress Publishers, 1972.

Bol'shaya Sovetskaya Entsiklopediya. 22+ Vols., Moscow, Publishing House of the Soviet Encyclopedia, 1970+.

L. I. Brezhnev, *Za ukrepleniye splochennosti kommunistov, za novyy pod"yem antiimperialisticheskoy bor'by (For Strengthening the Solidarity of the Communists, For a New Rise in the Anti-Imperialist Struggle)*, Moscow, Politizdat, 1969.

Yu. P. Davydov, V. V. Zhurkin, and V. S. Rudnev, eds., *Doktrina Niksona (The Nixon Doctrine)*, Moscow, Nauka, 1972.

I. Geyevskiy, *S.Sh.A: Negrityanskaya problema (U.S.A.: The Negro Problem)*, Moscow, Nauka, 1973.

Marshal of the Soviet Union A. A. Grechko, *Vooruzhennyye Sily Sovetskogo gosudarstva (The Armed Forces of the Soviet State)*, Moscow, Voyenizdat, 1974.

Yu. Isayeva, *Labirinty voyennogo biznesa (The Labyrinths of Military Business)*, Moscow, Mezhdunarodnyye Otnosheniya, 1969.

I. Ivanov, *Caution: Zionism!* Moscow, Progress Publishers, 1971.

A. A. Kvinitskiy, *Protivolodochnoye oruzhiye i yego nositeli (Antisubmarine Weaponry and Its Carriers)*, Moscow, Izdatel'stvo DOSAAF, 1973.

G. M. Kuzmin, *Voyenno-promyshlennyye kontserny (Military-Industrial Concerns)*, Moscow, Nauka, 1974.

M. I. Lapitskiy, *S.Sh.A: Rol' profsoyuzov vo vnutripoliticheskoy zhizni (U.S.A.: The Role of the Trade Unions in Internal Political Life)*, Moscow, Nauka, 1973.

Colonel General N. A. Lomov, ed., *Scientific-Technical Progress and the Revolution in Military Affairs,* translated by the U.S. Air Force, Washington, D.C., Government Printing Office, 1974.

M. Maksimova, *Economic Aspects of Capitalist Integration,* Moscow, Progress Publishers, 1973.

S. Menshikov, *The Economic Cycle: Postwar Developments,* Moscow, Progress Publishers, 1975.

V. M. Mil'shteyn, *Voyenno-promyshlennyy kompleks i vneshnyaya politika SShA (Military-Industrial Complex and U.S. Foreign Policy),* Moscow, Mezhdunarodnyya otnosheniya, 1975.

I. I. Mints, et al., *Sionizm: teoriya i praktika* (Zionism: Theory and Practice), Moscow, Politizdat, 1973.

Ye. D. Modrzhinskaya and Ts. A. Stepanyan, *The Future of Society: A critique of Modern Bourgeois Philosophical and Socio-Political Conceptions,* Moscow, Progress Publishers, 1973.

L. N. Moskvichov, *The End of Ideology Theory: Illusions and Reality; Critical Notes on a Fashionable Bourgeois Conception,* Moscow, Progress Publishers, 1974.

V. Mshveniyeradze, *Anti-Communism Today,* Moscow, Progress Publishers, 1974.

A. A. Popov, *Gosudarstvo i profsoyuzy* (The State and the Trade Unions), Moscow, Nauka, 1974.

I. T. Rogovskiy, *Politicheskaya ekonomiya kapitalizma* (Political Economy of Capitalism), Minsk, Publishing House of Belorussian State University, *imeni* V. I. Lenin, 1975.

P. A. Romistrov, Chief Marshal of Armored Troops, *Vremya i tanki (Time and Tanks)* Moscow, Voyenizdat, 1972.

Major General V. S. Ryabov, ed. *Dvina (Dvina)* Moscow, Voyenizdat, 1970.

Yu. Sevost'yan, *Planirovaniya vneshney politiki v S.Sh.A. (The Planning of Foreign Policy in the U.S.A.),* Moscow, M.O., 1974.

I. L. Sheydina, *S.Sh. A.: Fabriki mysli na sluzhbe strategii (U.S.A.: "Think Tanks" in the Service of Strategy),* Moscow, Nauka, 1973.

Yu. Shvedkov, ed., *S.Sh.A: vneshnepoliticheskiy mekhanizm (U.S.A: The Foreign Policy Mechanism),* Moscow, Nauka, 1972.

V. D. Sokolovskiy, *Soviet Military Strategy,* New York: Crane, Russak and Co., Inc., 1975. Edited and translated by Harriet F. Scott.

V. Zorin, ed., *S.Sh.A: Studenty i politika (U.S.A.: Students and Politics),* Moscow, Nauka, 1974.

Marxism-Leninism on War and the Army, Moscow: Progress Publishers, 1972.

Lenin: Selected Works, 3 volumes, Moscow: Progress Publishers, 1970-71.

Karl Marx and Frederick Engels: Selected Works, 3 volumes, Moscow: Progress Publishers, 1969-70.

The Fundamentals of Marxist-Leninist Philosophy, Moscow: Progress Publishers, 1974.

For Soviet broadcasts and monographs unavailable in their original forms, Foreign Broadcast Information Service and Joint Publications Research Service translations were utilized. As can be noted above, many monographs have been translated and published in English-language versions by Progress Press, a Soviet state publishing house. However, these translations provide only a very limited sample of open literature in Russian on the issues concerning this study, and it must be recognized that they represent works officially approved for foreign dissemination.

Index

ABM (antiballistic missile), sites 14;
  treaty 13-14
Acheson, Dean, 17
AFL-CIO (American Federation of Labor-
  Congress of Industrial Organizations),
  62, 65
aircraft carrier. *See* weapons systems
Air Force, United States, 112-113, 114;
  F-111A, 113; Huey Cobra helicopter,
  107; Kiowa helicopter, 107; precision
  guided munitions, 110-111; C-5A, 113
  B-1 bomber, 78, 113; F-15, 113
Aleksandrov, I., 44n
Aleksandrova, V. A., 65n
alliances, 91; predicted collapse of NATO,
  33-36; North Atlantic Alliance, 98;
  Western alliance, 100; military
  alliances, 92
America, 11; global role, 23; and the
  Third World, 36-43
American, 11, 17; American foreign
  policy and Soviet views, 11-23; foreign
  policy problems, 11; opinion of scholars
  of Soviet studies, 12n; American-
  Japanese relations, 34-35; American-
  Chinese relations, 46; American-Third
  World relations, 47; class struggle, 63-
  65; trade union movement, 64-65;
  American economic crisis, 85; youth,
  65; American military power, 87-127
  passim; aircraft, 111-114 *passim*
Andreasyan, R., 41n, 42n, 99n

Andronov, Iona, 82n
Angola. *See* FNLA; MPLA
anticolonialist movement, 24. *See also*
  national liberation movement
anti-communism, 61, 71; and Zionism,
  72-73
antiwar movement (in the U.S.), 67;
  demonstrations in the U.S., 69
Antonov, A., 36n, 66n, 98n, 99n
Arabs, 4, 82, 144-145; Arab East, 36, 99;
  Arabian Peninsula, 94; Arab-Israeli
  War. *See also* October War; Yom
  Kippur War
Arbatov, G. A., 60, 63n, 75n, 85n, 101n,
  122n
arms race, 69
army (Soviet), 107, 108-119 *passim*;
  All-Army Conference of Experts on
  Combat, 117
army (U.S.), 107, 108-119 *passim*; U.S.
  combat capability in the Vietnam War
  118-119
Atlantic Ocean, 97
Australia, 97
Babich, Colonel V., 112n
Babich, Yu., 81n
Bagrov, I. R., 74n
balance of power, new, 26
Bay of Pigs disaster, 1
Belaschenko, Captain First Rank T., 119n,
  120n